JUNOON

Pooja Lamba Cheema

INDIA • SINGAPORE • MALAYSIA

ISBN 979-8-89067-995-6

I take the liberty of dedicating this book on behalf of Shri Brajesh Chandra Mishra to his late wife, Rama Mishra, his soulmate, partner and confidante of sixty two years. The poem below seems apt for two souls who shall forever be conjoined in love.

KABEER

I am the inebriated love, why should I be conscious
Whether free or in world, why should I be bound?

Those separated from their beloved are wondering
My love is within me, for me there is no looking for him

The whole world keeps fighting over the name
I have Lord's name on my lips, why should I care for the world?

Not a moment my Love is away from me nor am I from my Love
I am in love with him why should I be perturbed?

Kabeer, the essence of love, is to remove duality from heart
If one has to walk a tender path, why to carry heavy burden?

I would like to extend my thanks to the entire Mishra family for their warmth, support and affection and especially to Brajesh Chandra Mishra for unknowingly being a great inspiration to me and giving me the opportunity to write his memoir, of which I loved every moment. I shall also always cherish his blessings, because I know the strength of his benisons.

The following autobiographical poem Muflisi encapsulates the life and essence of Brajesh Chandra Mishra. It was read out by him for the first time in 2008 in Lucknow on the occasion of the inauguration of his Management and Engineering College.

MUFLISI

Meri muflisi ne mujhko jeena sikha diya
Har zakhm killaton ka seena sikha diya
Pehran phati hui thi phir bhi shikan nahin thi
Paiband se hi asmat dhakna sikha diya
Gurvat ke aalamon main thi fikr kahan mujhko
Faakakashi ke dard ko sehna sikha diya
Toofane gardishi mein manti rahi diwali
Mohtaziyon ne jashn manana sikha diya
Dardon ki dosti mein befikr ji raha tha
Dardon ne hadd se bhad kar hasna sikha diya
Mohtaziyon se seekha thode mein guzar karna
Katre se humko dariya bharna sikha diya
Gaurav hai mera bharat
Pehchaan bharti hai
Hai karm meri pooja
Shramshakti aarti hai

No translation can truly do justice to the beauty of this poem, but I shall try:

My poverty taught me the art of living
I learnt how to mend my brokenness
My clothes were worn, but remained unwrinkled
I patched together my dignity
Where did I have time for worry in such impoverishment
What concern could I have when I was starving
I celebrated even as I navigated storms
Because I found everything within nothingness
I found happiness even in pain
My endless worries taught me how to smile
Destitution taught me survival
And helped me attain fulfillment while having nothing
I am proud to be Indian, proud of my identity
Work is my worship
Effort is my religion

CHAPTERS

PREFACE

ROOH

I first saw B. C. Mishra at his house when his wife's body was brought home from the hospital where she had been in intensive care for more than a fortnight, hanging precariously between life and death. The atmosphere in the palatial bungalow was somber but not melodramatic. There was no grieving or crying, just a grim silence as the members of the family tried to absorb the finality of her death. I never had the privilege of meeting the matriarch of the family: I have subsequently heard so many inspiring stories of the formidable lady that I wish I had, but I am glad I was at least able to glimpse her as she lay bedecked with flowers on her bier in the centre of the living room. I remember looking across the room to where the menfolk had gathered away from the women to decipher who her husband was. I could not immediately guess, since there didn't seem to be a distraught widower amongst them, but I finally conjectured that it was the gentleman who sat composedly in a chair, talking inaudibly to the people around him. At that time, I knew nothing about their marital relationship or how much he had doted on her throughout their married life. He looked very calm and self-possessed, but that could have been because societal norms prohibit overt displays of grief from menfolk.

I turned my attention back to the young-looking woman on the bier and the silently grieving relatives surrounding her. I seemed to be the only outsider there. We had recently developed a close friendship with the son of B. C. Mishra and also lived in very close proximity to their house.

It was tragically ironic that this happened on the very auspicious day of Diwali, the festival of lights. I had been wearing an orange silk outfit with ornate jewellery to celebrate with friends when the son texted those two unforgettable words to us: *Lost her.*

The finality of death. All of us had all been hoping and praying that our friend's mother would recover. Every day I would try to lift our friend's flagging spirits with words of hope and encouragement but hope is never a guarantee against loss.

As I gazed at the inert body on the bier, I reflected at the fact that at least the family members had the opportunity to bid her goodbye. I had not been that lucky. My parents had disappeared in a deluge some years ago and I have wished many times since then that I had had the privilege of lighting their pyres to bid them a final adieu. Lighting the pyre of loved ones is not an easy task, but not being able to perform their last rites is worse; almost a sacrilege.

She looked very peaceful. There was no sign on her face of the ordeal she had been through in her last few days. I felt awkward sitting there amongst people I did not know, but empathized completely with their loss.

SANJOG

I did not meet the protagonist of this book till a few months after this incident. The family had been looking for someone to author his biography because he had expressed his desire for a memoir. Perhaps it was his way of coming to terms with his loss and the fact that bereavement makes us contemplate our mortality. His son proposed the idea to me, but even though I was intrigued by all the stories I had heard about his father, I was apprehensive about authoring his biography. I was aware that I did not conform to the traditional and conservative setup of their family and hence the synergy required for the biography might be missing. Also, the narration would be in chaste Hindi and I am infinitely more comfortable with English. However, my misgivings went unheard because the family invited me over for lunch one fine winter afternoon with the general assumption that I was going to be chronicling their patriarch's life.

My first impression of the head of the family up close and personal was different from what I had expected, even though I knew by then that he was neither feeble nor irresolute. He was waiting for me on the porch of his palatial bungalow which overlooks a magnificent garden. I was taken aback by how young and handsome he looked, with no strain of the recent bereavement evident on his almost unlined face.

He directed me to the wicker chairs on the porch and without bothering with any preamble, launched into random incidents from his life. As I have said, I already knew some of them from his son. He did not direct his conversation entirely towards me. I sensed that he was not entirely comfortable with me, although he has three daughters who are roughly my age. I didn't mind, for I too was a little intimidated by him. I took this opportunity to study the man instead and listened carefully to the narration, lest I miss any detail. I looked again for signs of grief or despondency on his face, but I could not find any. Either my protagonist was an unusually strong man, or he was masterful at disguising his emotions from the world.

After a while, it felt too warm in the sun and I shifted to another spot which was partly in the shade, but B. C. Mishra did not shift from his sunny spot. Summer was coming in early and it was already promising to be brutal, I reflected.

When the family, who had respectfully stayed away during our tête-à-tête, summoned us in for lunch, the gentleman finally fell silent but did not immediately rise from his chair. Then, leaning back, and almost as if in soliloquy, started reciting a Hindi poem. It was a beautiful poem, even though I did not understand some of the words and it seemed somehow to poignantly encapsulate his life. I immediately thought it would make a lovely prologue for the biography. After he had finished, I asked who had written it and he replied with his first faint smile that it had been written by him. This was fantastic, I thought to myself. My protagonist was not only a formidable, inspiring character, he was also a poet! I then asked if he had written any more poems but he just shrugged and said that there might be some more if his wife had saved them, but since none of them had yet been through her personal effects, he did not know.

I instantly wanted to comfort the proud and resilient man in front of me and tell him that it was not unnatural at all for the bereaved to not be able to immediately handle sensitive and painful tasks such as these; it sometimes takes forever to be emotionally ready to tackle such projects. In my case, I never did become ready to handle my parents' belongings, eventually leaving them to my sibling to claim them. Their house remained virtually untouched for two years after their deaths, as if waiting to be reclaimed by its owners: some potted plants on the balconies still thriving and flowering, my mother's cosmetics still on her dresser the way they used to be, her everyday handbag in its usual place on a side table and my father's worn white pajamas still hanging from a hook in the bathroom.

I knew only too well the raw wound of loss, expressed so poignantly by the Lebanese poet Kahlil Gibran long ago:

"Your pain is the breaking of the shell that encloses your understanding. Even as the stone of the fruit must break, that its heart may stand in the sun, so must you know pain."

Even though I wanted to express empathy, I did not have the words or that level of familiarity with the elderly gentleman yet and he probably would not have appreciated the intrusion into that aspect of his life anyway.

He finally stood up and we followed him into the dining room, where the family was dutifully waiting for us. Lunch was an elaborate, vegetarian affair. His son and one of his daughters sat at the table with us. The daughter looked worried and did not eat, probably because her husband, a District Magistrate who had met me briefly when I arrived at the house, had left hurriedly owing to an incident of massive flooding in an area under his jurisdiction. It was being reported on television that many lives had been lost and that the situation was still grim. I tried as I ate to not think about floods and deaths and the passing away of my parents in similar circumstances eight years ago. To reflect too much was to risk slipping into despair.

SRISHTI

It was a crisp February morning when I visited my protagonist's college and farmhouses for the first time. The curved building of the Management and Engineering College had a red exterior and looked very imposing. His son gave me a tour of the college with its grand robotic labs and conference rooms, but what I especially loved was the vast wilderness behind the main building and the little pond there; a charming environment for the students of the college.

From the college, we drove to the cattle shelter owned by the family, with its prize bull and cows. Its lush green environs were another testament to the family's love for nature. Peacocks foraged peacefully in the periphery of the fields surrounding the cattle sheds.

Lastly, we visited the farm which B.C. Mishra had first bought after he closed down his transport business: a plot of land which had not been arable then because of its salinity, but which his wife and he made cultivable by hauling three hundred truckloads of Press Mud to it from a friend's sugar mill and with toil and diligence, grew thousands of mango and eucalyptus trees on it.

The farmhouse that was subsequently built on the land amongst the groves of trees was a white, colonial-style building, an excellent place for evening soirees. And I was told that soirees did take place there for several years; gatherings which hosted large numbers of influential people from in and around Lucknow. No sign of that bustle and revelry remains in the quiet and peaceful surroundings of the farm today. Even the pretty little cottages built some distance away from the main farmhouse building stand quiet and deserted. They were originally built as a getaway resort but B. C. Mishra had got disgusted with the venture when he realized that his numerous guests did not expect to pay for the hospitality there as they were used to the parties at the farmhouse. Plus, some of them, he later realized, were using the cottages for certain disreputable acts which greatly violated his ethics.

On our drive around the village of Sesendi where the college and farms are located, his son also pointed out another sprawling farmhouse a little distance from the road and told me that his father had bestowed it to his wife's brothers who he had raised like his own children when he could barely sustain himself and his wife. It looked so stately with its tall trees waving in the wind and I wondered at the extreme generosity of the man who apparently had many hidden virtues.

Before this visit, we had also toured the locality of Rajendernagar where the family resided for many years before they shifted to their bungalow in the cantonment. They had owned two huge houses there and one of them still had a plaque with the name B.C. Mishra on it, even though the houses had been sold long ago. I asked his son why it was so. He laughed and said that his father's name still carried a lot of weight in those parts and the owner probably thought it a good idea to retain the name because of it.

Rajendarnagar is an old neighbourhood and there is a famous restaurant there that serves Indian specialties. While we ate lunch there, the son told me an almost unbelievable story. "We used to come here a lot when we were kids," he said. "In those days, it would always be packed with customers. One day, my parents came here for lunch. They were not served for a long time and my father became furious. He told off the waiters, but they seemed nonchalant and even replied insolently to him. Perhaps it was because the place was so popular that the owner had become rather arrogant. My father stormed out of the restaurant with my mother, but he could not overlook the insult. He had powerful connections in those days and he got the owner of the restaurant arrested and let it be known to him that he had done it. The owner realized he had offended my father and sent supplications to him to get him released. My father's minions told the owner that my father had been disrespected in his restaurant and that he would only agree to have him released if he waited on him the next time he visited the restaurant."

"And did that happen," I had asked, quite aghast. "Oh yes," the son laughed. "And he was forever humble after that."

And this is the man whose biography I am being asked to write, I think to myself.

KARM

It was another sunny winter afternoon when I met B. C. Mishra for the second time. He had sent his car to fetch me from home. I sensed that he was still a little disconcerted at being alone with me, but he had to resign to the situation. We sat down on the porch facing the garden. I tried to make myself as benign a presence as possible, though my natural flamboyance is not easily suppressed. I just hoped the elderly gentleman would soon get comfortable with my presence and I with his.

Fortunately, Brajesh Chander Mishra is not a man who is easily intimidated by anything and since he is a keen talker, we were soon immersed in his stories. After a while, he did not seem to care at all that I was alone. I had carried a Dictaphone with me and I slid it as close to him as I could. He did not acknowledge the presence of the gadget and it seemed as if he did not like the conversation being recorded, but he said nothing.

Tea and snacks arrived but remained untouched because the protagonist was deep in his reminiscences and I was equally absorbed in listening to them. After a while, his granddaughter appeared and sat down beside him. She listened to him for a while and then left. A little later, his youngest daughter emerged from the house with her young son. She was tall and strikingly pretty, just like the granddaughter. She is also a renowned Doctor. She smiled and waved to me and said she was taking her son to the dentist. I smiled back and nodded. Her father did not seem to have noticed the intrusion at all and did not pause in his narrative. The third member of the family who made an appearance was one of his grandsons, who came into the porch and respectfully touched my feet. I hurriedly blessed him and turned my attention back to the head of the family, who did not care to be interrupted.

The only time he did allow his attention to be diverted was when a man bearing some gifts approached him deferentially. He asked the man who the gifts were from, and I heard the man saying the word 'didi.' I thus assumed the gifts were from his eldest daughter, who stayed close by. He gesticulated to the man to place the gifts on a chair and then reached into his pocket to take out a wad of notes. He handed some over to the man who had brought the gifts and then called out to one of his servants, telling him to place a few of those gifts in the car which would be dropping me home. "Also pluck a big bag of vegetables from the garden for didi to take home", he further instructed him. I did not know how to respond to this unexpected generosity and clearly, the gentleman did not expect any thanks. After the man who had come from 'didi's' place had left and the servant had also hurriedly disappeared to do as he had been instructed, my protagonist told me who the gifts were from. "There was a man who was involved in litigation with me over some land which was rightfully mine," he said. "He passed away recently due to Covid. Since he had been a thorn in my side for a long time, I had wished him ill-luck and as Providence would have it, my wish was granted. To the astonishment of his wife and daughter, I attended his funeral and also handed over the deed of the disputed land to them. They could not believe their eyes. The next day, they both arrived at my house with presents for my entire family: sarees for the women and dhoti kurtas for the men. They told me they were overwhelmed by my kindness. These gifts have also been sent by them."

This was the second example I came across of the incredible generosity and magnanimity of the individual whose story I had been commissioned to write. I would learn later, as we progressed in the biography, how philanthropic and altruistic he was, and how humble. I learned the details of this particular story many months down the line from his family members: details that he had probably omitted because he is a particularly modest man and a stoic who understood very early on in his life the transience of material things and that it is only our actions that determine the quality of our life.

The elderly gentleman ruminated ruefully over the fact that he had done wrong by wishing harm to someone and that there was always a price to be paid for any malintent. What he said resonated completely with my own belief in the laws of Karma, which I have expounded in my first and third books, but I did not interrupt him. He continued, saying that he had always wondered why one person remains in penury throughout his life while another is born or ascends to great riches till a family priest explained to him that one's fortune in the present lifetime is influenced by past deeds of previous lifetimes. Quite true, I thought to myself, and was glad that the elderly gentleman and I shared the same spiritual belief.

As the conversation progressed, the harsh rays of the winter sun lost their ardor and the afternoon turned into evening. I once again reflected on how young the hero of my book looked and the fact that his eyes were an unusual grayish-blue colour. I thought it was time I took my leave and I asked him if we should continue the session another time. He did not answer directly but reached for a little notebook that had been concealed on his person. From it, he took out a copy of a clipping from The Times of India. It was dated December 11, 1999, and titled 'Honesty Pays,' with his picture on the top left corner of the article. I skimmed the article and realized that it encapsulated his journey from a penniless thirteen year old to a very successful and prominent member of society.

I asked if I could keep the clipping with me for future reference and he answered that it was for me. I folded the clipping neatly and put it in my bag after which his stately chauffeur ferried me home along with a big bag of fresh vegetables and some of the gifts that had arrived earlier that day.

Once home, I mulled over the old man's reminiscences, his authority as the redoubtable head of his large family, and his incredible composure despite his very recent loss.

DUA

My third meeting with B. C. Mishra was once again at his sprawling house. This time, he was waiting on the terrace outside his private quarters, dressed in a smart suit for work. Two large marble lions graced the corners of the terrace as if forbidding any unwelcome entry. He asked me whether I would like to sit in the garden or on the terrace and I answered that I would be happy to sit anywhere, although I secretly hoped he would select a shady spot, as the sun had proved to be quite harsh on the two previous occasions. Fortunately, he led me to a beautiful, sheltered spot in the gardens in front of his private quarters. These were not visible from the front of the house, but I had once been taken on a tour of the bungalow by his son and lovely granddaughter and I had especially loved these gardens. Unlike the perfectly manicured front garden, it had more character with its many gazebos and profusion of ornamental plants. I had been told that the late matriarch would spend most of her day in these gardens among her beloved plants.

Co-incidentally, the spot that he chose for our session was a little clearing under the trees with verdant foliage which had been her favourite spot in the garden. The beauty of the place was further enhanced by the antique-style furniture placed there under a canopy of trees which lent it a whimsical charm.

As I was about to sit down, I was startled to see the two ferocious pets of the family, a beautiful American Akita, and a gorgeous French Mastiff, tied up not far away from us. I wondered why they had not started a frenzied barking at my arrival, but realized that the paterfamilias probably had a very sobering effect on them.

I barely had time to fumble with and switch on the Dictaphone and push it across the table towards him before he commenced with his narrative, stating that he would now start his story from the very beginning and proceed henceforth in chronological order. I assured him that I preferred a chronological narrative, considering that all my memoirs have been written in the same style.

Before he could continue, his granddaughter appeared once again and asked if I would like some tea or coffee and I acquiesced to black coffee, although I had just finished my lunch and am also really more of a tea drinker, which I prefer to sip slowly and alone in my dimly lit room while I mull over the complexities of life.

My coffee arrived along with some snacks. My gracious host insisted that I eat, despite my pleas at being rather full after my lunch, but I could sense that he would be offended if I did not and gingerly picked up one of the homemade laddoos (an Indian sweet) that were placed before me. It was delicious and I almost wished I hadn't confessed to being sated.

I learned that the gentleman would be narrating the period of his life from infancy up to the age of five today and I almost heaved a sigh of relief at not having to sequence the many random incidents that had already been narrated to me into a structured timeline.

The daughter-in-law of the house appeared quietly in the distance. I was about to rise to greet her, but she gesticulated for me to carry on sitting. She sauntered across to a swing in the garden not far away, sat there contemplatively for a while, and then started perambulating around the garden, attending to phone calls. Aradhana is also a formidable personality like her father-in-law; she is the leader of the Congress Legislature party in the state; as much a firebrand in the state legislature as she is soft-spoken and gentle outside it.

Before I start chronicling the story of Brajesh Chander Mishra, I must describe what happened that day just before I left. At the end of our session, I asked him for his blessings to officially begin writing the book because I intended to start transcribing our sessions that very day. Characteristically, he did not respond or show any emotion but called out to his daughter-in-law and asked her to bring him a gold coin from inside the house. She did not question her father-in-law at all about why he wanted it and returned with a velvet pouch promptly. I realized what his intent was almost immediately but was still completely flustered when he placed the pouch in front of me. I managed to stammer that I had only wanted his blessings, but he said that certain traditions needed to be followed. The gold coin was a shagun, a symbol of an auspicious start. Not knowing how to react to this, I lifted the pouch with folded hands and thanked him, upon which he told me that a doctor had paid him a house visit many years ago for which he had paid him five thousand rupees and that he had told the doctor that he should treat the payment as a blessing and not as a fee because it would prove to be very lucky for him. The doctor soon went on to become the owner of a very large and acclaimed hospital.

"Now that you are associated with me," he said, "Wait and see where your fortune leads you." I felt a slight shiver go down my spine as if I was being baptized. Once back home, I placed the velvet bag carefully among my valuables, resolving to keep it with me forever, knowing instinctively that his benediction would work for me.

PHULWARI

The incredible story of Brajesh Chander Mishra started in a village in the Unnao district of Uttar Pradesh on October 20, 1940. His ancestors had migrated to Karachi in Pakistan and made a fortune in cotton there, but had subsequently returned to Unnao.

His father, he tells me, was a big Zamindar or landlord who had been bestowed thirty or forty villages by the British to collect revenue from farmers as was the norm in those days. The British would anoint a chosen few as Rajas, Talukdars, and Zamindars in villages for this purpose. The Ziledar, who collected Lagaan or cess on behalf of the Zamindar, and the Mukhtiar or chief official who dealt with legal matters relating to the same, were both relatives of his grandfather and they all lived together in large houses in the same village. His bua (father's sister) had been forced to return to the village because of marital discord and his grandfather had built a large house for her in the village as well.

"There was much oppression and wrongdoing against women back in those times," he says. "I have seen so many changes in my lifetime. I have seen annas and pies being converted into rupees (the coinage in use at the time when one rupee was equal to 16 annas), the introduction of the metric system, liberation from our colonial masters, and the abolition of the Zamindari system. Some of the Zamindars were brutal with their subjects when it came to collecting cess: they would have the tenants who were unable to pay tied to Neem trees and whipped. We were different, though, there was no savagery in our methods and perhaps that is why God has always been on our side."

"We never saw or felt any shortage or lack of anything in our childhood, because farmers from surrounding villages would bring milk, grain, and other provisions every day to the house of my grandfather, the Zamindar."

"I don't remember much from those early days," he says, even though he manages to recount so many incidents from his childhood that I am quite impressed. "I do remember festivals being celebrated with great fanfare in my village," he says, with his face unsmiling but aglow, probably because in those days there was very little by way of entertainment in villages except congregations at festivals.

"On the Gudiya festival, milk would be brought in lotas or mugs by the farmers to the Zamindar's house as an offering for the gudiyas and would later be distributed to the whole village."

(I have no idea what the Gudiya festival is and I read about it when I return home. It is a festival observed in the rural areas of Uttar Pradesh in the month of Shravan, roughly the month of August. It coincides with the festival of Nag Panchami, the day of traditional worship of snakes. One of the customs of the Gudiya Festival is that children beat dolls fashioned out of cloth. This probably originated in the olden days when dominant upper-caste male youths would beat young women of lower castes around the time of Nag Panchami to affirm either caste or gender superiority. Fortunately, many years later, those young men started beating dolls using elaborately decorated sticks instead of hapless women at the Gudiya festival, perhaps because of the societal ramifications of such a practice on gender violence.

As to the origin of Nag Panchami, the month of Shravan was when the homes and holes of snakes would get flooded with rainwater, forcing them to come out into the open and people would offer them milk as a means of appeasement.)

"On Devuthani, mounds of sugarcane would similarly be brought into the village," he says. (Devuthani is celebrated to purify one's soul and prepare oneself towards attaining Moksha: salvation. The ritualistic practices associated with it are supposed to help human beings get rid of malefic planetary influences and attain happiness.)

"On Kartikeyi Purnima," he continues, his eyes softening at the recollections, "bullock carts bedecked with bells and streamers would arrive in the village and our entire family would go to the banks of the river Ganges to take a holy dip in its waters." (Kartikeyi Purnima is celebrated on the full moon day of the auspicious Kartika Month of the Hindu lunar calendar. For Hindus, the month of Kartika holds immense importance as it is the only month which is dedicated to the worship of both Lord Shiva and Lord Vishnu). "All of us children would eagerly await the festivals. The memories are hazy," he repeats, "but I remember my Mundan ceremony clearly." (Fortunately, I know what a Mundan ceremony is. It is one of sixteen purification rituals in Hinduism. This ceremony is supposed to rid a baby of all negativity from the previous life and promote mental and spiritual development). "It took place in the temple of Chandrika Devi in our village. My father wore a pristine white shirt and dhoti for it. He always wore white and was always impeccably dressed."

"I was his favourite child," he remembers fondly, "perhaps because I was the most handsome and robust amongst all my brothers and sisters, although parents love all their children equally."

"How many siblings did you have," I ask him. "Four brothers and two sisters," he replies. "One sister had already been married, so there was one sister and four brothers in the house at that time, as well as the four sons and daughters of my paternal Uncle." "All in the same house," I ask incredulously. "It was a very big house," he replies matter of factly as if the fact should have been obvious to me by now.

"We had chairs and tables in our house in those days when that kind of furniture was not to be found in village homes. English officers would ride up to the house and sit in the chairs to address the problems and grievances of the village folk while we children would all enjoy the spectacle."

I can't help commenting that it is admirable how vividly he remembers all this. He shuns the compliment and starts telling me about the death of his father. "I was only about four years old," he says, "probably not even four. My father left us all in our maternal home in Hamirgaon in Rae Bareilley district a day before his death. I remember a messenger coming to the house with the grim news the next day and the wailing of the ladies that ensued, although, at that time, we did not know that our father had died. The import of it hit us much later. We were bundled into a bullock cart and taken back to our village which was eight hours away. When we reached, we realized my father had already been cremated. According to some family members, he had committed suicide by consuming poison because of an altercation with my Uncle and Grandfather over which brother would be allowed to leave the village and settle in the city."

"Perhaps that is why the cremation was done so hurriedly," he says. "My widowed mother did not even get to see her dead husband's face."

"My Uncle bought a plot of land and built a house on it in Kanpur and they shifted there soon after my father's death. He took up a teaching job there. We were left alone in the big house in the village under the care of my grandfather. My Uncle also took my eldest brother along with him, though they became estranged later on. My father's apparent suicide due to poisoning was never mentioned in the family again."

"Well, that's all I can remember from those days," he says. I nod my head. I can barely remember anything before the age of five. I have only a few prominent memories of a chronically suppurating arm and of having to walk gingerly in the corridors of my Kindergarten school to avoid it coming into contact with anything. After the sores and suppuration healed, I fractured the same arm by slipping on a wet verandah outside my house one cold February morning after insisting I be let out of the house to play. The arm never healed properly and I was left with a permanent bend in it. This happened in the same house where we returned with our mother one evening after watching the movie 'The Little Mermaid' and saw our father lying in the garden with blood seeping from his head. He had had an accident while returning home on his scooter and for days we were as quiet as mice in the house because he suffered chronic headaches due to the injury to his head. I remember fearing he might not live.

I also remember wheezing and puffing my way through life because of my asthma.

I never forgot the movie The Little Mermaid because I was so mesmerized by the splendor and exoticism of a world under the sea and of the beautiful girl, half woman, and half fish, who had to relinquish her true love.

But I digress. The long pause in the conversation after the elderly gentleman says he cannot remember anything else means that the session is over. But I want to try and extricate some more details from his childhood. I prod him to tell me more. "Who were you closest to as a child," I ask him. It must have been pretty devastating for a little boy to lose his father so early on in life. He answers that till the age of five, he was hardly aware of what was going on around him, except mealtimes, which he remembers distinctly.

"We would help ourselves to arhar (pigeon pea) daal from a kathauti or wooden platter, which we would eat with thick rotis." Then his voice drops a fraction of a decibel as he considers my earlier question and says that he was close only to his father and after his death, there was no one else. "Perhaps only God," he reflects, adding that he did, however, become close to his family or rather more like a guardian to them, sometime in the 1990s.

In a much later meeting, I will learn about how he came to be a guardian to his entire family, beginning with him welcoming his young bride's eight-year-old brother who came with her at the time of marriage as dowry, he would laugh. He raised him like a son, even though the couple barely had enough money to get by. His wife's other two brothers also followed after a while and he became a de facto parent to all three of them.

What else shall I ask, I thought to myself, not wanting the meeting to come to an end. "What were your house and the village like?" I enquire. He perks up a little as if this question is at least more interesting than the previous one and says that the house was the usual type of large house you would find in a village. There was a well inside the house and three bathing areas, he tells me. The servants would fill water from the well for bathing as well as for drinking. His Uncle's family and his own stayed in two separate parts of the house. He traces a finger on the table to describe the layout of the house. He draws the two separate sections, the well and bathing area and the 'Mardana' and 'Zenana:' the parts of the house reserved for the menfolk and the womenfolk respectively. Then he outlines the area just outside the house where their cows and buffaloes would be tethered next to a pond, and then the 'phulwari' or garden and the wheat fields further beyond. I guessed that there was a Mardana and Zenana in Mishraji's house because the ladies of the house did not hobnob with the male visitors of the house.

"We would go to the phulwari with my grandfather in the morning to pluck flowers for the puja or prayers," he tells me, "and sometimes a little cucumber or gourd from amongst the vegetables that also grew there." Perhaps the flowers for the puja remind him of the family celebrating Navaratri (a festival held in honour of the divine feminine, occurring over nine days during the month of Ashvin, or Ashvina, usually September–October) because he tells me that there was a lot of pomp and show in the house on those nine days. "The families of the Ziledar and Mukhtiar would join us in the daily prayers and in the big feast on the last day of the puja, which was also held in my grandfather's house." "In olden times," he says, "a goat would be sacrificed during the festival," but elaborates that he only ever saw his grandfather slicing a huge ash gourd in place of a hapless animal during the festivities.

"These details are so fascinating," I tell him. In his usual un-reacting way, he shouts across to the grass cutters in the lawn who have been creating quite a bit of a racket nearby for a while now. "Do it tomorrow," he commands, and the noise stops immediately.

"We did not feel the absence of our father," he then volunteers to tell me. "Our lives revolved around our meals; always the thick rotis made of millet or barley and the pigeon pea daal. We never bought milk or ghee, because every large household in the village was self-sufficient in this regard."

That self-sufficiency continues to this day, I think to myself, remembering my visit to the huge Gaushala or cattle shelter owned by the family on the outskirts of the city and their prize bull, Nandu. I had a picture taken with Nandu, a fierce-looking magnificent beast who towers above most people, but is a gentle old soul.

"There were a lot of servants in the house," he now continues on his own. "They were not paid wages and their families would be given little parcels of land in lieu instead. Similarly, the labourers were not paid for harvesting the mangoes from the orchards, but were given a share of the harvest."

"There were many ponds in the village: separate ones for the Harijans (the untouchable caste) as they were then called, and the upper castes." He smiles broadly for the first time and says he used to love bathing in the ponds with his family because the canal water of the ponds was such a refreshing change from the well water in the house.

There is another pause and I know I have to fill it quickly before he calls it a day. All the childhood memories recounted thus far have been descriptive, but he hasn't shown any particular emotion associated with any of them. I set aside my inhibitions and asked him how his mother handled the death of their father. He answers dryly that she cooked and took care of the children and that there was nothing else for a widowed woman to do in those days anyway, but there is a faint glimmer of sadness in his gray-blue eyes when he says that widows could not wear anything except a simple white dhoti and blouse without any ornamentation whatsoever. At this point, I did not know that apart from everything else, the subject of my story was also a feminist.

I get a fleeting vision of his widowed mother in a white dhoti, going about the daily household chores with nothing more to look forward to after having untimely and tragically lost her husband. I further venture to ask about his relationship with his mother and he replies without any expression of filial love that she would make millet rotis at night (these were far more common than rotis made of wheat then, he informs me) and stack them up in the kitchen for breakfast the next morning and also give them milk in the evening. "Bas, aur kya tha," he says, dismissively, "What else was there?" "That was life: waking up in the morning, eating the basi (stale) rotis for breakfast with the daal that would have formed green edges in its wooden bowl by morning and would thus have to be mixed well before it was eaten; eating their afternoon meal of roti, daal and maybe a vegetable and eating an equally simple dinner at night."

"Chai, (tea)," he proffers, "only came into our lives much later, when small packets of it started being distributed in villages as something to add to milk. Before that, there was no concept of drinking tea." I know this to be true from my childhood visits to our village, where we were given unflavoured milk in big copper tumblers a couple of times a day.

For a brief moment, I am transported by those memories: the canals in which water glittered in the afternoon sun, peacocks in shady groves and the exciting expeditions to retrieve their fallen feathers, the wild berry trees, the enormous bales of cotton in the cotton ginning factory owned by us, my very sturdy and robust grandmother ruling the household with a heavy hand and the cows in the shed outside our own fortress-like sprawling village house, especially the two favourites I had lovingly named Star and Twinkle.

The stately man in front of me has lapsed into silence with a faraway look in his eyes as I remember my childhood. I wonder what he is thinking and I gently ask what he remembers of his father. His face softens into a smile and he reiterates that he was his father's favourite and was affectionately called Munne by him; a nickname which carried on, and that he even had a special song for him which he would sing often. He struggles to remember the song but cannot and says it will come back to him later. "My father was always humming around the house as he went about his chores," he says, his eyes still a little wistful.

I doggedly persist further in my questioning and ask what he remembers of his grandfather. Fortunately for me, he does not show any sign of irritation at my belligerence and describes how his grandfather would sit at the entrance of the courtyard of the house to receive the cess from the farmers. "He was also always dressed immaculately in pristine white clothes," he says, his tone revealing that his grandfather was a kind and benevolent man.

An hour and a half has passed, but I am not ready to give up enquiring into my subject's early life. I question whether his family was devout, considering that they are from the Brahmin or priestly class, but he answers obliquely that there were grand processions in the village on religious festivals and that there used to be great solidarity between Hindus and Muslims in those days. His countenance softens once again and I realize that memories of the festivals are probably the ones he cherishes the most.

"There were no daily prayers in our house," he now answers my question a little more directly, "although my grandfather would perform a little ritual before each meal in which he would light a little fire and offer some grain to Agni, the Fire God. Religion only really became prominent in my life after marriage," he says. I guess that the late matriarch was quite religious and it is obvious from the plaque that bears her name at the entrance of their bungalow how much she was respected.

"Some years into our marriage, I built poultry sheds on one of my farms and rented them out to a poultry farmer. A Brahmin relative asked me why I was abetting the rearing of birds for slaughter when I already had sufficient income from other enterprises and this made me reflect that it was indeed immoral. I closed down the poultry farm, even though the poultry farmer had given me advance rent for many months and I had to return the money to him. A few years after this incident, when I had become a big transporter, one of my trucks, which was specially designed for the transport of farm animals was regularly ferrying goats as cargo. I did not realize that I was inadvertently abetting in their slaughter as well. During one of the truck's trips to Calcutta, my son fell very ill. My wife rebuked me for ferrying live animals and said that I had invited misfortune into the family. As soon as the truck returned from Calcutta, I sold it. Miraculously, my son recovered immediately after. Whenever I have closed down any business which I felt was immoral in the slightest possible way, I may have incurred losses in the short term, but in the long term, I have always prospered because of it."

"I did transport animals in my truck after that," he smiles, "but it was Alligators that needed to be relocated from Kukrail Forest Reserve to Kalagarh Dam and they were in no danger of being killed. The children would always get very excited whenever they saw the truck with these creatures in it."

"In 1978, there was an auction of liquor vends in the city. The District Magistrate and the Superintendent of Police were friends of mine and they asked me out to lunch one day, with the request that we all travel together in my car because they did not want to be recognized. At lunch, they drank beer while I sipped water and revealed that they could help me get the licenses for the liquor vends. The liquor vends were highly lucrative, but I refused, knowing it would be unethical for me to deal in liquor."

This is how a man should practice religion, rather than chant or rant in the streets, I think to myself and these are perfect examples of Right Livelihood of the Eightfold Path taught by the Buddha.

"We were all quite naughty as kids and would often get hauled up for stealing gourds from fields or picking up goat kids from the herds of goats which passed in front of our house," he chuckles, the memory probably having surfaced because of the earlier story about goats. "I especially was a rogue and whenever I was scolded for any mischief, I would run away to the canal and have to be cajoled to return, often atop the shoulders of a family member."

"As a child, I was always popular with both the girls and boys in my village and this did not change in my adolescence in Lucknow, to where I was recalled by my family after failing my High School exam for the first time."

"Ten or twelve is an innocent, tender age. At that age, girls used to treat me as if I was Kishan Kanhaiya," he chuckles, referring to Lord Krishna and his Gopis. Gopi comes from the Sanskrit language and means cow-herd girl. In Hindu mythology, Gopis refers to the group of cow-herd girls who were known for their undying love and devotion to Lord Krishna. I can imagine the handsome elderly gentleman as a young boy: good-looking, intrepid, enterprising, and a bit rebellious: qualities that would have been highly appealing to the opposite sex.

I have now run out of questions to ask. I can only hope that more reminiscences from that time might surface later. What I did not know at the time was that my protagonist did not care much for childhood reminiscences because they were tepid compared to what transpired later in his life.

When I stand up to leave, he gallantly escorts me to the car which is waiting to take me home. Another car immediately pulls up to drive him to his office, where he still directs the workings of the large empire he created out of nothing at all.

MADHUSHALA

"Zindagi ke aakhri lamhein
Kuch is tarah guzre
Naa kuch hum samajh paye
Na hum kuch keh paye"

(The last few moments of life ended in such a way
that I understood nothing; that I could say nothing)

My distinguished protagonist starts our next session with these lines. I waited for him to proceed further with the recital, but none were forthcoming and he tells me that not only was his wife's death unexpected, he could not even bid a proper farewell to her as she did not want him to visit the hospital during the pandemic. "Go back home and look after the affairs of the house and the children," she would say whenever I visited and force me to leave. "Even the children would stop me from coming to the hospital. I often think about how, in the end, there was not even an exchange of words between my wife and me."

Today, we are sitting in his bedroom, probably because it is evening and also probably because the comfort level between us has grown by leaps and bounds. He is perched on a settee in the room dressed in a white kurta pyjama and I am sitting in a chair opposite him.

I ask him if the lines he has just recited were written by him and he replies in the affirmative. I ask him if there are any more lines to the poem and after a moment or two, he says:

"Mit ta nahin yeh lagawat ka silsila
Kabhi aahat pe kaan
Kabhi dar pe nazar."

(The yearning refuses to go away
I listen for the sound of your footsteps
I gaze at the door to see you appear)

"It's been three months since my wife departed," he tells me, "but I have not got used to her absence. When I am outside in the gardens, I feel she is inside the house and when I am indoors, I seem to always be listening for the sound of her footsteps."

I do not know how to commiserate with him because he has been extremely stoic all this while and can only say that it takes a long time to heal from bereavement.

A servant walks in and is told to open the drapes, even though it is dusk. The servant does as he has been asked and then bustles around the room, tidying up. Once the servant has left, he resumes the conversation by reciting the following lines:

"Aaj jo peeche mud ke dekha
Toh kuch yaadein bula rahin thi
Ab tak ke sare safar ki saari baatein
Bata rahin thi
Kitni mushkil rahein thi
Hum kya kar gaye
Ek sukoon ki taalash mein
Kahan kahan se guzar gaye
Kitne log mile safar mein
Kitne bichar gaye
Janmon tak saath nibhane wale
Jaane who kidhar gaye
Alag hi zamana tha who
Alag hi daur tha
Zindagi jeene ka maksad hi kuch aur tha

Bachpan ki naadaniyan thi
Khwabon bhari jawaniyan thi
Ghar ki zimmedariyan thi
Kaam dhande ki pareshaniyan thi
Har umar ke sapne alag the
Khushiyon ka drishtikon alag tha
Goal alag tha, mol alag tha
Aayine mein khud ko dekh kar sochta hoon
Kya khoya kya paya"

(I looked back today when some memories beckoned
They were narrating to me my life's journey
What I achieved, despite all odds
How I struggled in search of happiness
The people I met along the way
And the ones I lost
My dearest beloved, I do not know where they have gone
It was a different era
With a different goal in life
The innocent mischief of childhood
The dreams of youth
The responsibilities of a household
The struggles to earn a living
Different experiences in different ages
A different perspective on happiness
Of goals and success
Now, when I look at myself in the mirror
I ask myself what I have achieved)

I am mesmerised by the recital and can't help telling him that his poetry is of the caliber of a famous Indian poet, but in his usual diffident way he ignores the compliment and starts to play a song on his mobile, which I realize is set to one of his poems:

"Mujhe khone paane ka gam nahin
Kisi ranjo gam ka gila nahin
Rahe saath saath ye zindagi
Kinhi daulaton se yeh kam nahin
Mujhe khone paane ka gam nahin
Yoon toh hasratein bhi hazaar hain
Lage khwaishon ke bazaar mein
Hua haath haasil kuch nahin
Toh bhi aankh meri nam nahin
Mujhe khone paane ka gam nahin
Kisi ranjo gam ka gila nahin
Rahe saath saath ye zindagi
Kinhi daulaton se kam nahin
Mujhe khone paane ka gam nahin

Na tha humsafar koi paas mein
Raha rehnuma ki talaash mein
Mili manzilein hain yeh chah ki
Kinhi jannaton se yeh kam nahin
Mujhe khone paane ka gam nahin

Na toh zarzaron ka malaal hai
Nahi aandhiyon ka khayal hai
Main toh uss makam pe aa gaya
Jahan haadson mein bhi dam nahin
Mujhe khone paane ka gam nahin

Teri bandagi ka kamal hai
Teri har dua bemisal hai
Tu hi humsafar, humdum mera
Teri meherbani kam nahin
Mujhe khone paane ka gam nahin"

(I have no sadness over what I have gained or lost
I have no grudges or resentment
Our togetherness
Was more than any wealth or success
Even though desires are never-ending
In the end, I have nothing, but I am content
I had no companion
I searched for a guide
And I found the path of love
Greater than Paradise
I have no sadness for my struggles
No remembrance of the storms
I have reached a point
Where happenings cannot affect me
It is Your grace
Your benediction, your benison
You have been my companion
Your kindnesses have been limitless)

I am speechless after listening to the beautiful song with its lyrics aptly alluding to the stoic but not irreverent character of their composer, but when his daughter walks smilingly into the room and asks if I liked her father's poetry, I manage to answer that I am overawed.

"Mummy had a whole diary of Papa's poems," she says and asks her father where the diary is, but he does not answer and starts playing another song on his phone, probably to avoid having to think of his late wife's untouched possessions.

I recognized the lyrics of the second song instantly, which are from his poem Muflisi, which I have already introduced in the prologue to the biography.

The songs are even more beautiful than the poems if that is possible. "When did you start writing poetry, Uncle?" I ask him when the song ends. He answers that it was during a period of his adolescence spent in Nainital and Bareilley that he developed a love for live recitals. "The population there was predominantly Muslim and all gatherings would inevitably end up in Sher o Shayari (poetry recitation)," he says. "Hindus and Muslims lived in perfect harmony then. We would listen to songs and poetry almost every evening and dream of finding perfect love. This was in 1955-1956. We also used to watch a lot of films in those days and imagine that our future partners would be like the heroines in the films." He laughs softly and says that at least in his case, this did happen. He points to two youthful pictures of him and his wife hung side by side on the wall. "She is sixty years old in this photograph, can you tell?" he asks me. "No, not at all," I reply honestly, gazing at the picture of his wife in which she is looking away from the camera and smiling shyly. I then turned my attention to Uncle's picture and asked him how old he was when the picture was taken. "Sixty-one," he replies. I'm equally surprised by how young he looks and I tell him so. "Well," he says, shrugging aside the compliment, but much more at ease with me now, volunteers that there are far better pictures of him from that time, but since his children chose these photographs to display in the room, he did not object.

"Since the last ten years, however," he says with a rare display of humour, "whenever I look in the mirror, it is as if the mirror is laughing at me." I laugh and tell him that this is not true and I mean it. He is still a very handsome man, tall, and well-built, with blue-gray eyes, a fair complexion, and a steely countenance.

"When we got married," he carries on, "we both were very good looking and there was no couple in our circle of friends who could compare to us. She resembled the two popular heroines of the time,

Vyjanthimala and Asha Parekh, and I had modeled myself after my favourite hero, Rajinder Kumar." Oh, I think to myself, so that is who he looks like in the picture on the wall. Rajinder Kumar was one of the great thespians of the Indian film industry and when I was growing up, he was considered one of the best-looking actors. "Our love was unique in every way," he continues. "Once, when we were newly married, we had just returned home after watching a movie starring Asha Parekh, and my wife's younger brother was asked if he knew who the female lead in the film was. 'Asha Parekh of course,' he replied and received a playful slap. 'You idiot, it is your sister and you don't even know it!'

We both laugh together and he informs me that a well-known tantric from Benares who had recently passed would always address his wife as Vyjanthimala ever since their first meeting in 1990.

"I would also be called Rajender Kumar," he says abashedly, "because I styled myself after him. I would wear my tie just like him and don the same sunglasses." Then, probably thinking he has been immodest enough and that we were not supposed to be talking today about his life beyond the age of five, he reverts to where we had left off last time.

"After my Uncle left for Kanpur, my grandfather and widowed mother were the only elders left in the house. My Uncle asked my eldest brother to come and stay with him in Kanpur because he was fond of him. Besides my mother and grandfather, it was just me, my two brothers, and my unmarried sister in that big village house. Zamindari had not yet been abolished, so we still did not lack for anything. Medical science, though, was very nascent and there was no known cure even for fever. Whenever any of us kids were down with fever, sabudana (sago) would be boiled in water and given this concoction to drink in the belief that this would bring the fever down. When we contracted chickenpox, however, there was nothing to be done but sprinkle Neem water on us and wait for the infection to subside."

"After some time, my Uncle called our entire family to Kanpur," he says, and then suddenly pivots from the conversation to start playing another song on his phone. "The other day, I showed my youngest daughter the video of this song and asked her if the actress in it didn't look exactly like their mother. Here, come and see," he beckons to me. The heroine in the video is neither Asha Parekh nor Vyjanthimala. It is Madhubala, the legendary heroine of Hindi cinema, the most classic and divine beauty of all with a face that reflected both innocence and playfulness.

"Did Aunty look like her?" I ask and he replies while the video continues to play that they often looked like replicas of each other and said that he would show me some photographs in which she looked exactly like the actress.

"Did she have long hair?" I ask suddenly. "Yes, very long hair," he replies, "and also those beautiful little curly side locks that were so much in fashion then."

Nostalgia and yearning flash briefly on his face and then he returns to his story. "I was seven years old when my Uncle called my older brother and me to Kanpur as well. My mother stayed back in the village with my youngest brother and unmarried sister."

"In Kanpur, I received more attention than both my siblings and my cousins. My Aunt loved me very much. She would favour me even over her sons and daughters. Unlike the village, life in Kanpur was not easy. There, we had always had plenty to eat. My Uncle was just a teacher in Kanpur with a modest salary. When their house was being built in Kanpur, my Aunt would often pitch in with the labourers so that they could save some money, but nothing dampened their love for city life."

"No buses plied those days, only trains. There was only one train from Kanpur to Rae Bareilley and the train station was about eight kilometres away from my Uncle's house. To reach our village, we would first take a bullock cart to the station. The train from Kanpur would reach Rae Bareilley at night, from where we would hire another bullock cart to take us to our village. By the time we reached the village, we would sometimes be fast asleep with exhaustion. There was no dinner for us after we reached: this newfangled culture of eating a meal at any time of the day or night did not exist then."

"Food was strictly rationed in the Kanpur household, but my Aunt always ensured that I ate well. The other children did not fare as well and were often scolded for demanding an extra paratha at mealtime. She was undoubtedly very fond of me. Every morning, before daybreak, the two of us would set off for Bhairon Ghat (quay or landing steps next to the water) on the river Ganges, a long way from our home in Arya Nagar. There was nothing but fields in between and we would walk through them to reach the Ghats. I am sure that today there would be nothing left of those fields and that the area must now be a bustling locality."

"I would carry my Aunt's cloth satchel for her. After we would bathe in the Ganges at Bhairon Ghat, my Aunt would give me two pice or half an anna to spend on a snack at the stalls there. That amount was enough in those days for me to be able to choose from a wide array of snacks."

I can visualize the narrator as a young boy hopping and skipping through fields, bathing and splashing in the Ganges, and looking forward to that day's snack; some of the simple joys of life at the time.

"We, my Aunt and I, carried out this morning ritual in all seasons and we would always return home before sunrise so that my Aunt could get started with her household chores. Again, there was no concept of either morning tea or breakfast for any of us. When tea was first introduced in our village, probably for the British officers, it was such a novelty that it was poured out from a ladle into bowls and drunk that way; there were no teacups and saucers in those days. Our first meal of the day would be at about 9:30 am because my Uncle and his eldest son had to leave for work after that. My eldest cousin brother had been employed by the Reserve Bank of India. Back then, passing High School was enough to get good employment. Breakfast was always very basic and frugal. I know my entire staff eats way better than that today," he smiles.

"The evening meal, the second and last meal of the day, was unvarying: parathas with baingan (brinjal) curry, because brinjals were cheap. The brinjals would be sprinkled with salt and turmeric and the curry was just the juice of the brinjals that had oozed out."

"After dinner, we had to sit and study from six in the evening to ten at night. The bunch of us would huddle around an oil lamp with a tutor who stayed in my Uncle's house and taught the children in lieu of rent. None of us could dare to move from our places till the end of the study period."

"I remember the day Gandhiji was assassinated, 30th January 1948. My Uncle was very fond of sweetmeats and every evening, one of us was sent to fetch something or the other for him from the market. On that particular day, the child who had been sent on the errand returned shouting that Gandhiji had been killed."

"Honestly, as children, we cared nothing for his martyrdom and celebrated the fact that our study session that day had come to an abrupt halt. Schools also shut down the next day. For us, this meant freedom from studies and the luxury of being able to roam around throughout the day. In the park opposite our house, an Akhand Kirtan (continuous singing of devotional songs) of Raghupati Raghav Raja Ram had started and it went on for days (Raghupati Raghav Raja Ram is an excerpt from the hymn 'Sri Nama Ramayanam', originally composed by Lakshmanacharya. A modified version of the composition was made popular by Gandhiji). We boys would often go there to hang around and would only return home when we were really tired."

"Our school in Kanpur was rudimentary. There were no tables and chairs, only reed mats on which the students would sit. Our notebooks were tablets of wood, which were polished with the sides of glass bottles to make them smooth and we would write the alphabet on them. There was a song about these wooden tablets with the words Chandan (sandalwood) Ki Patti, which we would listen to as we diligently polished our tablets."

He laughs at the recollection and I laugh too, amazed at the simplicity of those times and compare the uncomplicated songs of those days with the senseless stuff that usually passes for lyrics now.

"Well, this is how I spent a year of my life in Kanpur, by which time a school had been built in our village on land donated by my grandfather. It was decided that we brothers would go back to the village to study in that school."

Before he can proceed with the story, his daughter-in-law comes into the room and greets me in her soft, sweet voice, quite unlike the one she uses when someone, usually a belligerent opponent, needs a good tongue-lashing. Her father-in-law tells her to eat something from the array of snacks that are always laid out for me, as if I may be in danger of malnourishment. She says she is tired after her trip to her constituency but consents to eat a bit of the Rasmalai because she has quite a sweet tooth. After that, she bids us goodbye and leaves the room.

Resuming the story, Uncle says that they came back to the village and started studying at the school there. "We stayed there for two or three years. Meanwhile, my eldest brother had fallen out with my Uncle and had left Kanpur to go live with my married sister in Lucknow. It was nice being in the village during the summer holidays. My Uncle's family returned to the village every summer. Distinguished people such as Harivansh Rai Bachchan would visit our village from time to time. I have personally heard him reciting Madhushala near the railway crossing in our village." (Harivansh Rai Bachchan was an Indian poet and writer of the Nayi Kavita literary movement of early 20th-century Hindi literature and Madhushala, his best-known work, was part of a trilogy inspired by Omar Khayyam's Rubaiyat, which he had earlier translated into Hindi).

"In 1950, however, our circumstances changed drastically. The Zamindari system was abolished. Our days of prosperity came to an abrupt end. The farmers stopped paying tax to the Zamindars, but the government was still collecting cess from us. To try and protect the family's honour, my mother decided to sell her gold bangles and told my grandfather to accompany her for it. We immediately sold one of our buffalos as well. Thus started an era of Patan for us: downfall or collapse."

"By then, trouble had also started brewing among my family members. Quibbles were happening regularly between my Uncle's family and my own over trivial issues especially relating to the children. Then we heard a rumour that my Uncle was planning to get my brothers and me murdered without a thought for my grandfather who was still alive. Soon, we started seeing unfamiliar faces in the village, which filled us with foreboding. Frightened that the rumour might indeed be true, my family and me huddled into a bullock cart one night and left the village. My second sister had been married off by then in the neighbouring village to a Junior Engineer, also called Overseer in those days, with the Irrigation Department. At the time of our escape, he was posted in Sambalpur in

Orissa, overseeing the building of the Hirakud Dam on the Mahanadi River, but she was in her husband's village with her in-laws."

"The bullock cart took us to the station, where we caught a train for Unnao. At Unnao, we boarded another train for Lucknow and finally reached the house of my elder sister. It was a three-bedroom house, in which only my sister, her husband, and my eldest brother had been living. Having nowhere else to go, we moved in with them."

"But I should stop here," he says, to my disappointment. "We are only supposed to talk about my life till ten years of age. Plus, I do not want you to get bored." Although I protest that I can't get bored with his captivating stories, he says we should call it a day.

As I walk out of the room, I encounter several members of the family sitting in the living room. His eldest daughter Madhulika, who is married to a senior officer in the Indian Railway Services, has come to visit her father, and the rest of the children are there as well: Mrinalini, Malvika, and Ambika, along with Aradhana and their daughter. There had been a fourth sister Meenakshi who was born after Madhulika, but she passed away tragically at the young age of fifty-one after a long battle with lung cancer. She had also been married to an officer in the Indian Administrative Services.

The women of the family are all very beautiful, I muse: tall, slender, fair, and blessed with sharp features, including the granddaughter Nandaja, who stands five feet ten inches in her stockinged feet and looks like a mix of Selena Gomez and Jennifer Lawrence.

It is quite the family reunion in the living room and I find myself unwittingly in the midst of it, although it is an opportunity to acquaint myself with the progeny of the man whose biography I am writing.

The atmosphere in the living room is somber. I gather that it must be a rare occurrence for all the children to be present together in the house away from their busy schedules. The conversation is subdued as they recall bittersweet memories of her omnipotent presence. At that moment, her absence in the living room is almost palpable. She was the glue that held the whole family together, managing all the affairs of their large household.

While I am engrossed in the stories, their father walks into the living room. I have been so mesmerised by his poems and the songs set upon them that I request him to play 'Muflisi' once again. He does not seem to mind my request and all of us spend the next few minutes listening to the song, silently mulling over our trials, tribulations, and tragedies.

JUGNU

In our next meeting, the Paterfamilias continues his story from the time he was ten years old. "My problems were only just beginning. My eldest brother did not like me at all because I was the only one who would stand up to him and he would beat me often. At the end of that summer, he decided that I would be sent back to the village, not only for my perceived insubordination but also because my family was worried about their share of the property in the village."

"I was only ten years old, but it was assumed that I would be able to stay alone in the village and fend for myself. My Aunt was in the village at the time with her two daughters-in-law, but I had received strict instructions to stay away from my Uncle's family, so I could not even eat with them. My Grandfather's sister, for whom he had built a palatial house after she returned to the village also refused to have anything to do with me, because she did not want to anger my brother in Kanpur."

"I had never lived by myself. The first night alone in our section of the house, I felt very frightened and lonely. I could hear the calls of wild animals and I did not sleep the whole night. The next day, I walked to the neighbouring village to look for my sister. Fortunately, I was able to find her and she gave me food to eat. I began living with her, but I still had to attend school back in my village, so I would eat my morning meal of parathas and subzi at my sister's house and then set off for school with three or four other boys from her village. We would return in the evening and my sister would give me my evening meal."

"Despite the hardships, we were like any other mischievous boys our age," he says with a smile. "When I tell my grandchildren some of the stories of mischief, they laugh a lot, like the one where we would steal sugarcane from the fields. Four or five of us boys would stand on the edges while one would sneak into the field and break off a stem of sugarcane. If the snapping sound alerted the owner of the field, we would start clapping and shouting to warn our friend inside and then all of us would make a run for it with the sugarcane," he laughs. "Then we would merrily walk home, each sucking on a piece of the sugarcane, extremely proud of our daring."

"We would also steal cucumbers," he laughs again, "and we had an ingenious method for doing so. One of us would pretend to sit down in the field to defecate but would be tying a string to a cucumber. Then we would walk out of the field innocently, with the farmer being none the wiser. When we were some distance away, we would pull at the string and the cucumber would come trailing behind us! However, our intrepidity came to an end one day when the farmer saw a cucumber trailing away from his field. He chased us almost all the way home!"

"Then came the time for our High School exams. The norm in those days was that the elders in the villages would allow boys from other villages to stay in their houses to take the exams if the exam centre happened to be in their village. Anyway, I failed my High School exam. It wasn't surprising because there had not been anyone in the village to force me to study. In my summer break, I went to Lucknow to my family, and they decided I'd better start studying in Lucknow so that I could reappear for and clear my High School exam."

"Well, I was admitted to DAV College in Lucknow to prepare for my exam. I was nearly thirteen years of age, but I barely had any clothes and had to go to school in a simple shirt and underwear. All the boys would make fun of me. I decided something had to be done to rectify the situation and started tutoring the two daughters, aged six and seven, of a Sikh gentleman for eight rupees a month. My family did not know about this, because I used to walk to their house immediately after school, tutor the girls for an hour, and then return home. With my first salary, I bought cloth to get a pair of pajamas and a shirt stitched. In those days, one would get about two and a half metres of cloth in just one rupee. I also bought a detergent bar to clean my new clothes. I was still left with about two or three rupees. My eldest brother still disliked me and would not miss a single opportunity to berate or belittle me. When he saw my new clothes, he asked me where I had got them from and went into a rage when I told him about the tuition. He slapped me hard, asking how I could have kept the money for myself while he alone was earning for the entire household. The next day, I stopped the tuition. I realized that there was no point in earning any money if I could not spend it on some necessities."

My heart almost bleeds at the ingenuity of a thirteen-year-old boy receiving not praise but punishment and at the unfairness of it all, from being sent off to live in the village on his own and then being recalled to a life of constant criticism and abuse.

"It was a summer night when the result of my second attempt at the exam came out. I was lying on the roof of the house. The High School and Intermediate exam results used to be a very big deal. Even when they were declared at night, newspaper vendors would run through the neighbourhoods shouting the news."

"As soon as I heard the commotion, I ran down and purchased a newspaper. I looked for my roll number in the list of candidates who had scored Third Division (the lowest grades in the erstwhile marking system), but it was not there. I thought I had failed and went despondently up to my room, where I extinguished the oil lamp and lay down. Not long after, my elder brother entered the room and after giving me a hard kick on my back, proceeded to give me a good thrashing, shouting all the while that I was a liar and cheat who was playing games with the family by not telling them that I had secured a Second Division. I had not bothered to look at the Second Division list because I could not imagine doing any better than the passing grade!" Surprisingly, this incident is narrated without any rancor.

"The same thing happened when the result of my daughter Malvika's Super Specialisation exam was published in a newspaper. I scanned the entire list but could not find her roll number. I thought that she had not made it, but my daughter-in-law, who had been peering at the newspaper over my shoulder, joyfully congratulated me for Malvika having stood third in the exam in the entire state. I must have looked confused because she pointed to the three roll numbers highlighted at the top of the page. Her roll number was the third one from the top."

"That one year in Lucknow was very difficult for me because of my brother. I was getting beaten frequently by him over the most minor transgressions, more so because I refused to be cowed down by him."

"I had been given the duty of going to Qaiserbagh or Aminabad once a month to buy fruit and vegetables for the house. They were both a long distance from the house and I would have to walk all the way there and back, hauling a huge bag of produce. Each time, my brother would inspect the purchases and invariably find fault with something or the other. One day, I could not take it anymore and asked him why he didn't just do the shopping himself as I was so clearly inept at it. The beating that day was more severe than usual."

"I had enrolled in the first year of college by then and become a very good student. Teachers were writing praises for me in my notebooks. This motivated me greatly and I started studying even more diligently. My brother still thought of me as a failure, though. One night, I was studying by the light of the oil lamp in my room when he walked in. Snatching the book from my hand, he asked if I was studying or fooling everybody by pretending to study. I do not remember my reply, but he went out and returned with a thick Neem twig, with which he flogged me mercilessly. Finally, he told me that he would not be supporting me anymore and that I should look for a place to stay as he was throwing me out. I replied defiantly that I make my arrangements and this angered him so much that he flogged me again, saying I would end up a beggar. 'I may end up a beggar but I will never beg you for help,' I told him. 'And if I ever do come begging to you,' I added, 'slam the door in my face."

"The flogging was so bad that I could not sleep at night because of the burning and stinging. I had livid scars all over my body. Nobody came to commiserate with me. Even my mother never intervened, because, just like the other members of the family, she was both dependent on and afraid of him."

"That night was the last straw. The next morning, I went to school as usual with five rupees which were left over from the grocery money. After school, I handed the books and my NCC-issue shoes to a good friend of mine, telling him to drop them off at my house. The books would fetch some money for my family and the shoes were the property of the school. Then, with only the five rupees in my pocket, I made my way to the railway station, from where I boarded the Sealdah Express to Bareilley. I knew that the sister who had taken care of me when I had been sent to the village was now in Bareilley with her husband and young son because he had been posted back to his home state after his tenure in Orissa."

"I reached Bareilley in the evening and hired a rickshaw for eight annas to take me to my sister's house. Upon reaching the house, I learned to my dismay that they had been posted out of Bareilley. I asked the rickshaw driver to take me back to the station. This cost me another eight annas. I slept on a metal bench at the railway station that night."

"The next day, I walked aimlessly around the station, worried about what would happen to me, but determined not to return to Lucknow. A Muslim gentleman enquired what I was doing alone at the station. I replied with all the confidence I could muster that I was looking for a job, although I was afraid to be put to some lowly menial work. The Muslim gentleman must have noticed that I was quite well-groomed and enquired further about who I was and where I had come from. Upon learning my story, he asked if I had any money and whether I had eaten. I told him I had run out of money and had not eaten anything since the day before. He immediately ordered a glass of tea and a packet of savories for me from a nearby shop and I ate it ravenously. I still remember the taste of it. Then he sent me with one of his men to a nearby hotel, where I was served a platter of food with six chapattis, rice, daal, subzi, and chopped onions and chillies. I have not forgotten that meal either," he says and I can imagine how it must have tasted to a famished thirteen-year-old who did not know where his next meal was coming from.

"It was a veritable feast for me," he says, "a starving boy who had not eaten for two days. I ate till I could eat no more and there was still some left over. I was then taken to the house of the Muslim gentleman and given some blankets and a place to sleep. The next morning, he asked me what work would suit me and I replied that I would do any kind of work. 'And what wages would you like,' he asked, and I asked him in turn how much he could give me. 'Will forty rupees do?' he enquired and I happily agreed to the amount, for it was quite a sum of money in those days, especially for a penniless thirteen-year-old boy like me. He took me to a Railway Overseer and arranged with him for me to inspect the railway wagons which would arrive in Bareilley every day with construction material for the Dhaura Reservoir near Pilibhit. As it happened, the Overseer knew my brother-in-law and told me where they had been posted. He also said that I did not need to work for the Muslim gentleman and could work directly under him instead. This is how I became a work-charged or contractual employee. The Overseer began paying me fifty rupees a month: ten more than the Muslim gentleman had offered. He said he had added the extra ten rupees for my food. I was also given lodging in the sprawling offices of the Rohilkhand division of the Irrigation department."

I am transfixed by this story of the boy who would not tolerate injustice and left his home with barely any money to face an unknown and daunting future.

As if reading my thoughts, he says, "It wasn't easy living on my own. I bought an Angeethi (clay stove) for a rupee and a half, a Tawa or flat pan, and Babool (Acacia) twigs for kindling for the stove. I tried making chapattis, but they got burnt each time and I would cry while eating them. Sometimes, I would soak them in sugared water to soften them and make them palatable or I would just eat raw carrots and sugared water. I missed home a lot and sometimes wished I had not left, but I always knew I would never return after what I had told my brother."

"I could not go back home and I could not kill myself, even though I did contemplate going down to the railway tracks and ending my sorry life many times. The only option left for me was to carry on and face whatever adversity came my way."

Perhaps the thought of suicide was abhorrent to him because of the mystery around his father's death, I thought to myself but did not share this thought with him.

As if reading my mind, he says, "I did tell my wife a few years ago that we were done with all our worldly business and there was no reason for us to continue living. I told her to get me my revolver and said I would shoot her first because I did not want her to die a widow and then myself. She scolded me for saying this, but of course, I did not mean it seriously. If I did not choose to kill myself when I was completely destitute as a thirteen-year-old orphan, what reason was there to take my own life when I had my partner and family with me?"

"I guess my determination to not give up helped me. Karma and Bhagya (Action and Destiny) go hand in hand. My brother-in-law was posted back in Bareilley in place of my supervisor less than a month after my arrival there. Now I had both a job and a family and a servant to cook our food. I even hired a bicycle for eight rupees a month. After some time, though, my brother-in-law advised me to try for a better job and told me to go to Roorkee to meet his friend, who would help me get one. So I went to Roorkee and stayed there for about two weeks but it was evident that my brother-in-law's friend did not have any employment for me, although he was nice enough otherwise. Every day, he would order tiffin for both of us, and in the evening, we would listen together to Binaca Geet Mala (an iconic musical program on All India Radio which was started in 1952 and which was the first version of what later evolved as the countdown for songs based on their popularity)."

"Since there was no work for me in Roorkee, my brother-in-law's friend finally sent me back to Bareilley with a tattered blanket for the train journey. Over there, I was once again assigned work-charge duty. After a few days, the job was proving to be quite monotonous but once again, I got lucky because the SDO (Sub Divisional Officer) of the construction division had become my friend and he suggested a job that I would find more challenging. It was in Pilibhit, where the Dhaura and Nanak Sagar dams were being constructed. These two dams were very large projects started by the Indian Government and they were in a very nascent stage. There was a large requirement for labour there. People debate the pace of development in our country after Independence, but I can tell you from personal experience about the rapid progress that took place in the Terai (the Terai is a strip of undulating former marshland running along the lower ranges of the Himalayas) on the infrastructure front after Independence. The Dhaura reservoir and Nanak Sagar dams were built by Indians and provided electricity to thousands of villages."

"I soon left for the jungles of Pilibhit, which at that time were still being cleared to build the dams. There was no accommodation there; just tin sheets placed on top of brick columns and fires were lit at night to keep wild animals away. Food was not a problem, however, as the management ran a langar (community kitchen) for the workers."

"I was assigned to soil testing, which meant that I had to excavate soil using a pipette in the entire area up to a depth of a few feet and list the types of soil in the samples. These samples would then be sent to Roorkee for further testing. In most places, the soil was usually clay and coarse and fine sand. Clay was used for building the dams. All these huge dams were built using manual labour and mules which would ferry the materials from one place to another. The mules were so essential that the more mules a person owned, the more work he could get. The status of the contractors was thus directly proportional to the number of mules he had," he laughs.

"It's such a fascinating story, Uncle," I tell him. "Well, I am only narrating dry facts," he says, "it is really up to you to flesh out the story and make it interesting enough to read."

"Well, since I was more educated than most of the other workers, the SDO called me one day and told me to make a report of the types of soil in the area," he goes on. "Not only did I make the report, but I also drew a map detailing the different borings, the strata of soil, and the samples of soil that had been obtained. He was most impressed with my work and commended me, saying I was almost an engineer. He forwarded the report to Roorkee and I earned a promotion. From a daily wage earner, I became a work-charge supervisor, with a regular pay of seventy-five rupees a month. Of course, I had to take an exam for it. I was only fourteen years old then; it had only been a year since I had run away from home and I had spent six months out of that in the jungles."

Fourteen, I muse; an age where the kids of today would barely be able to manage their schoolwork!

"But were you not the youngest worker in the area?" I ask. How did you manage to oversee those much older than you? Did they not resent it?"

"Well, they were only labourers," he replies, "and also I was well-liked by everyone because after all, I was only a little boy and I would also do odd jobs for everyone. I had nothing else to do after my official work was done. Plus, everyone knew that I was close to the SDO, who was the boss of the place. A lot many of the workers would often call me and give me some treat or the other so that they would be in my good books and I would not tell the SDO what tricks they were up to," he laughs.

"One problem almost arose when a distant relative of the SDO landed up in the area, looking for a job. It was assumed that he would take over my appointment. But I had proved myself worthy and the SDO was very fond of me, so when the Junior Engineer asked him if his relative needed to be appointed in my place, he refused and said that two appointments could be created for the same job. Perhaps that was a good thing because the SDO's relative was completely uneducated and not too bright either."

"What was the job of the Supervisor?" I ask him. He explains that after the soil brought by the mules was laid out on the earth, it was first flattened by machines called Graders and then compacted by huge rollers pulled by tractors. It was his job to see how much soil had been compacted. The contractors who did the compacting would try to save money by leaving the engines of the tractors running at night while the tractors remained stationary or were barely moved at all. The lights of the tractors and the sound of their engines would convince everyone in the camp that the soil was being compacted. The relative of the SDO was on the take with these corrupt contractors, making ten or fifteen rupees on the side each month. I reported this to the SDO, which angered the contractors greatly, but they couldn't do anything about it. I became even closer to the SDO and he started depending more and more on me."

"I remember one incident in the jungle as clearly as if it happened yesterday. The area was a complete wilderness and full of wild animals. (I can just imagine how it must have been more than sixty years ago, considering that even today, the area is populated with tigers). I was in a dense part of the jungle with four labourers and a leopard came charging out of the jungle towards us. Fortunately, we were not his target; it was a deer he was hunting, but he passed so close to us that it made our clothes flutter. We were left completely shaken," he smiles.

"There was another incident that I remember vividly. It was evening time and we were in a little clearing in the jungle when we saw a tiger bring down a wild buffalo not far away from us. Normally, wild animals would keep away because of the fires we would light at night, but they had not yet been lit and so we were able to witness this frightening but also magnificent sight."

"We were not worried or fearful about the wild animals all around us," he says as if guessing what was on my mind, "because there were watchmen deployed in the camp and of course, the fires would keep them at bay. Also, the predators were not interested in hunting humans; prey was abundant. I would roam quite freely and fearlessly around the camp."

"The jungles were full of deer. Sometimes, when the Graders would be on the move in the jungle, I would hop on to one of them and watch the eyes of thousands of deer reflected in the lights of the Graders. That is all we could see in the darkness, and when the workers fired at the multitude of lights, we would know that a bullet had met its mark when one of those lights fell to the ground. Hunting was not prohibited in those days, so the men would sometimes shoot deer for meat. I was just a little kid hanging on to a Grader with grown-up men and their rifles, but no one would mind me coming along, because I was so amiable. Every afternoon, when I used to be out in the jungle overseeing the testing or compacting of the soil with the labourers, I would instruct them to pluck Falsa (blackcurrant) fruit from the wild Falsa trees that grew in the middle of the jungle. When I would return, I would crush the fruit for juice and then go around the camp, distributing the refreshing juice to everyone. I guess I really couldn't sit still," he smiles. This is so like the story of Mowgli, I think to myself. What a wonderful movie it would make!

"After a deer hunt, the deer which had been culled were brought back to the camp to be cleaned and cooked. Deer meat is salty," he informs me, and this is news to me, even though I have tasted it. "Did you eat the meat," I ask suspiciously and he laughs and says he did not; he was only told by those who did.

At a much later time, he tells me that he had to eat fish for a month while he was absconding for a false murder charge against him. I was both aghast (meat is sacrilegious for a Brahmin) and impressed at his practicality as well as his devil-may-care honesty.

"I have a photograph from those days somewhere," he smiles. "In it, I am sitting on rocks in the middle of the Baigul River on which the Dhaura reservoir was constructed. The rivers in the Terai were rain-fed and the dams were built to collect the rainwater brought down by the rivers for irrigation."

"By the time I was fifteen, asbestos dwellings had been constructed in the area for the workers and a temporary colony had been established. Each house had two rooms with attached bathrooms and the houses were separated by courtyards. There were cots in the rooms. Water, of course, was never a problem in the Terai region because one could dig a couple of feet anywhere and water would come gushing out. Each house had a hand pump, from which water was drawn. The unmarried supervisors shared houses, while the married ones stayed with their families, who had slowly started moving into the area."

"At the age of fifteen, I had a job, an income, a furnished house, and plenty of food, which I did not have to cook myself. And I had finally got pants and shirts stitched for myself and bought proper shoes."

"Were you happy in those days, Uncle?" I ask him. He replies that he never thought about whether he was happy or sad: he had enough to eat, work to keep him busy, and proper clothes and shoes; what else did a man want?

"Did you not miss home then?" I ask, trying to think like a fifteen-year-old who had been away from his home for two years. "Who was there for me at home?" he says. "All I ever got there was beatings. And I honestly did not miss my mother much. There was not that much closeness between us."

"Yes," I concur, "I guess families had far too many children in those days for any kind of closeness or indulgence." And, of course, times were hard and the pursuit of the necessities of life did not leave much time or energy for any sort of indulgence anyway.

"Why would I miss home," he reflects. "I was getting better food in the camp and had a much better life there. While the entire household back in Bareilley was running on the ninety rupees that my brother earned, I was earning seventy-five rupees all for myself. I did not have to pay rent like my family or spend any money on food, because of the free canteen there run by the government. I could save up my entire salary."

"You had no expenses at all?" I ask. "What was there to spend on there?" he says, but then remembers that he had started spending fifteen or twenty rupees a month on clothes and grooming essentials which were brought from the towns of Haldwani and Bareilley. I would get a few pants and shirts stitched every month and yes, also buy the best creams and powders that were available those days. I had everything a gentleman of those days could have: smart clothes and shoes, a comb, and the best brands of toothpowder, toothpaste, and soap available then. I would listen to the brands that were advertised on the radio and buy those brands," he smiles. I also smile broadly at this recollection, because I know how few brands were around those days. Even when I was growing up in the 70s and 80s, there was only so much in the way of choice of grooming products and cosmetics.

"I was rapidly coming into my own," he recounts. "I was already tall and fairly decent to look at (the diffidence quite evident once again) and had started carrying myself well. When I was off work, I would swagger around the campsite like an officer, dressed in my best clothes. I had also started imitating the heroes of films, parting my hair like them or walking and talking like them."

"Fate had suddenly turned kind towards me, even though I was away from home, estranged from family, and working in difficult conditions. In a year, I had gone from living under a tin sheet and being a daily wage earner to staying in my own house and becoming a supervisor. The campsite had been transformed into a settled colony with lots of families. Of course, it was still very primitive compared to how developed it became later. In 1980, I took my family to see my Karambhoomi (literally, region of work or activity, but symbolically, the place where one's good and bad actions reap karma), and I could barely recognize the area because of the permanent colony there and metalled roads which spanned the sprawling dam and the places where previously even bullock carts could not go."

"It was hard for me to describe to my family what the place and my life there had been like," he ends with a smile and a look in his eyes which make me think of the young lad who would go into the jungles at night to watch the enchanting sight of the eyes of deer glowing like fireflies.

KALPANA

"I used to think that I was fourteen years of age when I ran away from home till recently, when my granddaughter was playing Binaca Geet Mala for me and I told her to keep going back through the years till I came upon the songs of my early adolescence. We used to watch a lot of films in those days, as I told you, and I remembered some songs from the year 1954. It was then that I realized that I turned fourteen in October that year, but I had already left home in July, so I was only thirteen when I left."

"When I look at children who are thirteen and fourteen years of age," he muses, "I wonder how I managed to accomplish all that I did. I left home with a vow to never return and a determination to not kill myself either, no matter what the struggles. There was a Junoon in me, a passion, to achieve. I guess this was what kept me going and made me adapt to different circumstances and situations. But never in my wildest dreams did I imagine that I would reach a status in life where I would have high-ranking bureaucrats and a doctor as sons-in-law, a legislator daughter-in-law with a very famous parliamentarian as her father, or that my daughter would become one of the most acclaimed gynecological surgeons in the state and my son would become a highly successful businessman in his own right. I look around at my bungalow and its gardens and the fleet of cars and remember the little boy who ate burnt chapattis and tested soil in the jungles of the Terai and I cannot believe how far I have come. But, in the end, I owe all that I have achieved to my wife; to the role she played in my life, and the good luck that she brought when we got married. At the time of our marriage, I did not even own a cycle and hoped that I may receive one as a wedding gift from my in-laws, but they were as poor as I was and my dream of possessing one did not materialise."

He then takes me back to where we had left off last time, telling me that at sixteen, he was offered a permanent job as an SDC (Sub Divisional Clerk). "It was unheard of in those days for an underage boy to secure a permanent Government job and that too without going through the proper channels of selection. I got the promotion because of my honesty and integrity. At the time I started as a supervisor under the SDC, his stenographer was buying the monthly stock of stationery for the office. When I became close to the SDO, he assigned this task to me. The Stenographer had been overcharging for the stationery and pocketing thirty-five rupees a month. When he learned that I was to do the purchasing henceforth, he was afraid of his fraudulence being discovered and told me that I could keep overcharging and keep the extra money for myself. My immediate superior also told me to keep quiet and do what the stenographer had advised. However, with the very first purchase, I presented the right bill to the SDO, as well as the extra thirty-five rupees which I had been told to pocket, informing him of what had transpired between the stenographer, my superior, and me."

"The SDO was shocked by the deceit of his Stenographer. He told me to keep the thirty-five rupees and buy myself some new clothes with it. A month later, when he was sitting with the Executive Engineer in Kichha, the topic of a vacancy for the appointment of SDC came up and he told the Executive Engineer that he knew of a very loyal, honest, and hardworking boy who he felt could be given the appointment and shared this story with him. The Executive Engineer wrote a letter of recommendation to the Superintendent Engineer to appoint me as SDC. Luckily, someone working in the household of the Superintendent Engineer also knew me quite well and vouched for my honesty and diligence. He suggested to his employer that the Department could start my pension two years after it was eventually due since I was only sixteen and two years underage for the job."

"This is how I was appointed Sub Divisional Clerk at the age of sixteen: the very appointment under which I had initially trained as a work-charge employee. The SDC had been posted out since then and the man who had been appointed in his place was both lazy and dishonest, which is why the Executive Engineer and the SDO had decided to hire someone else in his place. My salary now became ninety rupees a month."

"However, I felt I had been unduly rewarded for only doing the right thing and wrote a letter of resignation to the SDO. The SDO simply tore up the letter of resignation when I presented it to him, saying I should get on with my work and let him get on with his."

"Everything went well until the SDO was transferred out and a corrupt Mohammedan was appointed in his place, accompanied by his Chaprasi or errand boy, who was also from his community." He pauses to urge me to eat the mithai which has been lying in front of me for a while. I have not eaten any of it because I am not hungry and I also do not want to add the extra calories to my waistline, but he insists, telling me it is a delicacy made of moong dal (lentils) which his daughter got back from Bareilley. I cannot refuse and pick up a piece. As with all the snacks served each time, it is delicious and I inwardly smile at getting to sample so many specialties of the state of Uttar Pradesh at their house.

At that moment, Mrinalini, who brought the mithai from Bareilley, walks into the room and greets me fondly. Her husband has recently been posted back to Lucknow from Bijnor, where he had been the District Magistrate. I travelled to Bijnor a few months ago and received very special treatment as the District Magistrate's guest. The husband and wife had taken me to visit the remarkable Kalagarh dam and the reserve forest nearby, where an elusive tigress emerged from the dense foliage to grace me with her presence. Mrinalini, a brilliant hostess, had also laid out huge scrumptious spreads for her guests.

She tells me that it is difficult for her to be back in Lucknow with her mother not being there anymore and then updates her father on how the repairs on their allotted official accommodation are coming along. She asks me how I have coped through the mayhem of the last few months: Covid has hit all of us quite hard, and I tell her about the friend I have recently lost. She tells me that they lost both her mother-in-law and her sister-in-law's husband to Covid. Her father suddenly interjects this somber conversation to ask her if she remembers the family trip to Dhaura reservoir. She replies that she has faint memories of it because she was only ten years old at the time. He tries to jog her memory by describing how a hare being chased by a predator had jumped out from the jungle near the Inspection house and she smiles and says that she does remember that particular incident.

We are silent for a while after she leaves. "So what happened with the Muslim SDO, Uncle?" I finally ask.

"Yes," he says, snapping out of his reverie. "The Mohammedan SDO would delay the payments to the Hindu contractors even after the bills had been vetted by me, whereas the few Muslim contractors who were there would immediately get cheques even before their bills had been vetted. This unfairness did not sit well with me. The SDO's flunky was also getting on everyone's nerves because he would speak in an insolent manner and behave as if he owned the place. This was because the SDO and he were thick as thieves and they would even eat their meals together like friends. We all decided that we needed to do something to rectify the situation. Since I was the boldest and strongest among us all and known for my deep moral conviction, I was designated as the head of a conspiracy to oust the corrupt SDO and his errand boy."

"We knew about a corrupt practice of the SDO which could get him into great trouble. He used a Muslim contractor to dispense petty cash and cheques for him. These were carried by the contractor in a chest on a bullock cart, guarded by a Dafedar and four or five sepoys. There were two keys to the chest. One would be with the SDO and the other with the Dafedar."

"One day, the SDO handed about twenty-eight thousand rupees to the contractor before proceeding on leave. We persuaded the Dafedar, who was Hindu, to also take two days' leave on the pretext of his brother being seriously ill. After he left, we sent a telegram with my signature to the Executive Engineer, the District Magistrate, the Superintendent of Police, and the District Treasury Officer in Bareilley stating that the SDO was misusing Government funds."

"Telegrams were considered ominous in those days," he laughs. "Whenever anyone received a telegram, wailing and crying would begin in the household even before the telegram was opened because it was assumed that it contained bad news. But they were still the fastest means of communication. Letters would take four or five days to reach and there were no telephones for long-distance communication. Local communication was also rudimentary. Telephones those days had old fashioned dials, in which each number was dialed by rotating the dial a corresponding number of times."

"In response to the telegram, a raid was conducted and the SDO was recalled from leave. The chest was opened in front of the Chaprasi and when it was discovered that there was cash missing from the cash chest, the SDO was arrested and imprisoned."

"Four or five days after that, I was transferred to the Head Office in Bareilley. There, a farewell function was organized for the SDO I had previously worked under. In that huge gathering, one of the senior officials stood up and announced that the relationship between the SDO and his clerk was sacrosanct and should not be violated, indirectly stating that the incident that had recently taken place should not have happened. Furthermore, he said that the activities within a Division were a private affair and that making them public was an offense. I could not believe what I was hearing and immediately jumped up and asked if reporting corruption and theft was an offense. I would have said more, but the SDO told me to sit down. I obeyed, but was simmering inside at the implied accusation and support for the unscrupulous activities of the organization."

"A few days after this transpired, some Junior Engineers in the Division asked me if I wanted to continue as a clerk. 'If you continue here,' they said, 'you will remain chained to a desk and at the most, you will retire as a senior clerk.' 'Well, what should I do instead?' I asked, already quite disillusioned with the state of things and the lack of real challenges in my present job. 'Why don't you start a contracting business for yourself,' they suggested.

"The idea started appealing more and more to me as the days went by, but I did not have the seed money to set up a contracting business. However, when the Sub Divisional Clerk under whom I had originally trained came to know what I was considering, he offered me some capital, saying that I could return it whenever I wanted."

"I had been staying with him and his family ever since I had come to Bareilley. I was very close to him and he treated me like a younger brother. His widowed mother, three brothers, and sister were also very fond of me. I used to call his mother Mata (mother). We would eat our meals together like I was a member of the family, with the communal bowl of subzi laid out on a charpoy (cot) and Maa serving us hot chapattis from the stove. The sister knitted beautiful sweaters, always embroidering them with a pattern of two roses and a leaf in contrasting colours. She knitted one for me as well. She also embroidered sheets and pillow covers with the same design and tasseled borders. In those days, most girls would sew and embroider, but she also attended college and was very good at academics. I was quite in awe of her. Once I cut my finger and Mata told her to bandage it for me, but when she approached with the bandage in her hand, I became so nervous that I extended the wrong hand!"

"One of the brothers, who had taken to drink, started resenting my being treated as a member of the family. One night, after a bout of heavy drinking, he started questioning his mother why she treated me like a son and told her it was not proper for me to stay in their house with their unmarried sister."

"I heard this argument and was deeply aggrieved. I was very principled, and could not bear a slur on my character. However, I realized that I was eighteen, a grown-up man in those days, and did not want to cause the girl or her family any embarrassment. I have told you that I was very influenced by the heroes of films, who were honourable and gallant. I was wearing suits and ties and sunglasses like them and even my black and white shoes were inspired by a movie star. I also wore my hair with a side lock on my forehead as some of them did. I was an avid movie watcher. Sometimes, I would watch up to four shows in a day! But all the movies were about failed love affairs: there was never a time that one did not emerge from the theatre crying. Not that I had any romantic feelings for the sister, but this further convinced me that I should move out of the house lest any such situation should ever arise."

"This was also a love story that failed, except that there was only failure here and no love," he laughs.

Then he says he probably should not be relating such things to me, but I smile and tell him it reveals his strength of character, sense of honour, and his resolve.

"I shifted out of their house and started staying in a one-room accommodation on the premises of the Head Office, which had been officially allotted to me. I did not stop visiting the family; I would go over once in a while to have a meal with them. Mata was saddened and asked me why I had moved out of the house and I told her that I would have had to move out eventually anyway, but at least I was visiting and still eating meals with her. The other brothers also missed me; in fact, they had objected to my leaving, but I could not compromise their sister's reputation.

She eventually moved away, to China, I think," his voice trails off.

"After I left Mata's house," he continues after a while, "I would often remember the lyrics of a song and sometimes even sing it aloud while riding my bicycle to work":

"Jin rahon pe tum milte the
Un rahon pe chalna chod diya
Badnaam na hone denge tujhe
Tera naam hi lena chod diya"

(It's hard for me to translate these lines into English, but their essence is 'rather than let any dishonor come upon your name, I have stopped traversing the paths on which we would meet, I have even stopped taking your name to protect your honour').

"Was this a song from a film?" I enquire. "Yes," he replies. I tell him I want to know which song it is and he starts searching for it on his phone.

After several attempts, he manages to find the one he was looking for and reads me the lyrics of the entire song:

"Jiss dil mein basa tha pyaar tera
Uss dil ko kabhi ka tod diya

Badnaam na hone denge tujhe
Tera naam hi lena chod diya

Jab yaad kabhi tum aaoge
Samjenge tumhe chaha hi nahi
Rahon mein agar mil jaoge
Sochenge tumhe dekha hi nahin
Jo dar pe tumhare jaatin thi
Un rahon ko humne chod diya

Hum kaun kisi ke hote hain
Koi humko yaad karega kyun
Apne do aasoon bhi hum par
Koi barbad karega kyun
Uss manjhi ko bhi gila humse
Majhdhaar mein jisne chod diya
Jis dil mein basa tha pyaar tera…"

"Did you remain close to the SDC?" I ask, still impressed by his nobility. "Yes," he answers, "during the camp days, we not only worked together but also shared one of the asbestos huts. We had one cook and we would always eat together. It used to be quite cold in the Terai and our food used to mostly be meat and eggs and liquor." I am aghast hearing this and I ask if he ate meat and eggs as well, to which he answers that he did eat eggs and loved omelettes for breakfast! This is also quite shocking to me, not because I am vegetarian, but because eggs are also a sacrilege for Brahmins and I know that their household is strictly vegetarian. "I used to eat eggs every day for breakfast," he smiles, "in fact, I could cook very good omelettes." Good Lord, I think to myself, as if it is I who has sinned. Quite nonchalantly, he tells me that he used to drink as well. "Really?" I ask, quite horrified now, although I enjoy liquor myself. "Yes," he laughs unabashedly for once, "I did drink for a couple of years. I also smoked. I started at the age of seventeen. I was a chain smoker smoking about five packets a day of Wills Filter cigarettes. I used to have nicotine stains on my fingers. My wife made me quit smoking after we got married, though. She did not like how I smelled after smoking. Later, I quit drinking as well. After that, I never smoked or drank again. A family priest also told me before my son was born that I should not touch meat or eggs ever again and I never did."

I smile and shake my head at his candour. I could never have imagined him having any vices.

"So you quit smoking because your wife asked you to," I state with admiration. "Yes," he says. "We were strangers when we got married; both poor as church mice, but our Kundlis or astrological charts matched exceedingly well. Where my planetary influences were weak, hers were strong and where hers were weak, mine were strong. We made up for the deficiencies in our fates."

"While she was on a ventilator in the hospital, her face became more youthful and beautiful. Malvika commented to me on how young and pretty she looked, as if she had somehow managed to go back in time."

"You have seen her photograph at sixty-one years of age. Now imagine, if she looked so pretty then, what she must have been like as a seventeen-year-old girl."

I ask if I can see some more photographs of her and he tells me to go into the closet and see the ones there. I am a bit hesitant to enter the closet, which I feel is a personal space. Sensing the hesitation, he stands up and leads me into the closet himself, where two framed pictures adorn the wall. One is a wedding photograph and the other, he informs me, was taken twenty years after marriage. They both look young and beautiful in the pictures and the love between them is hugely apparent in the pictures. We walk back into the enclosed verandah adjoining the bedroom, where we have been sitting. Beyond it is the garden with the gazebos. I can't help telling him that I remember how young and beautiful Aunty looked as she lay on the bier bedecked with flowers the night they got her back from the hospital. "Were you there?" he asks me with surprise. "Yes, I came as soon as I heard," I answered. "Oh," he says softly, "then you have seen her...and how beautiful she was."

There are three things that I have come to greatly respect about the man whose memoir I am writing: his integrity, his pragmatism, and his undying love and devotion for his wife. Even though she is no more, she is always on his mind. He refers to her beauty and goodness and the unwavering support she had for him in almost every conversation.

"She was from a poor home and so was I. The Kundlis were matched for two people from poor families, but they matched so well that we could achieve what we both could never even have dreamt of. Her father worked as a Munim (accountant) in the court of the Raja of Sesendi. Sesendi was their village, where we later acquired hundreds of acres of land and built the college."

"From the time boys and girls are fourteen or fifteen years of age," he suddenly seems to change the subject, "they start getting attracted to each other. I have already told you that I was always popular with the girls, right from the time I was a little boy staying in my sister's village and was treated like Krishna. But I never believed in dalliances and thought that if I ever did have a romantic relationship, I would marry the girl. I was that upright. And to tell you the truth, I never courted women; it was always the other way round."

"I always wanted to marry the girl I fell in love with, and since I had an arranged marriage, I fell in love with her. 'Complete surrender for one another and living only for each other': that was my motto and it became hers as well. She taught me so much; I moulded her so much; we faced dire struggles together and we ended up achieving so much that today, we are like the rulers of the village where she grew up as a poor girl."

"The mangoes are being harvested at the farm," he digresses suddenly. "Why don't you go and see?"

"Have you gone there recently, Uncle?" I enquire of him and he says he has been there twice to supervise the sale of the harvest this season. Then, after some quick mental math, he informs me that this year's harvest has crossed 1500 quintals of mangoes.

"Wow!" I exclaim, "That is a lot of mangoes!"

"There was not even grass there when I bought the land," he tells me. I ask him how he dared to buy the land when it was not even arable and he answers that he had the courage because he had read the Mahābhārata (one of the two major Sanskrit epics of ancient India, the other being the Rāmāyaṇa), in which the Pandavas transformed the infertile land of Khandavprastha into the beautiful city of Indraprastha. I smile and almost shake my head in disbelief at his unbelievable resilience.

The story of Khandavprastha which he has just referred to goes like this: When there was a dispute between the Kauravas and the Pandavas over the division of the kingdom, Khandavprastha was given to the Pandavas and the rest of the Kuru kingdom was given to Duryodhana. Khandavprastha was a barren land of forests situated west of the river Yamuna, in what is now present-day Delhi. The Pandavas were not very happy with this decision, as the land was infertile. But Lord Krishna convinced them that they could transform the land into a beautiful capital for their kingdom and told them that Hastinapur, which had been the capital of the Kuru kingdom, was their Janambhoomi but Khandavprastha was their Karmabhoomi.

"Still, it was an act of great courage and faith, Uncle," I tell him. "See, when a man has been facing struggles almost since he was born, things stop daunting him," he says. "When I could run away penniless from home at the age of thirteen and start working in the jungles of Pilibhit, what was so intimidating about making a piece of land cultivable?"

"I have had to work hard all my life. When I set out to buy this house in 2000 (referring to his expansive bungalow), people thought I was mad. We had two big houses in Rajendarnagar and this house was in ruins. The walls were broken and some roofs were missing. Bats were roosting in the house. There was no garden or gate and a garbage dump stood where the chowk (roundabout) now stands. Cows and buffaloes would roam in the area. I got the garbage dump removed. The road in front of the house was narrow and riddled with large potholes, which would fill up with rainwater. Seventy trucks of sand had to be brought by our JCB dumpers to fill up the potholes. A few days after the road was repaired, I met an Army General at a friend's place who told me admiringly that I had worked wonders with the area around my house and that if it was up to him, he would allot all the bungalows in the cantonment to people like me."

There is a funny incident from this time which he narrated to me when we were almost finished with the book. His wife and he were both very fond of roses and one of the first things they did after they bought the bungalow was to start planting a row of rose bushes just outside the house. One day, he was hard at work with his trowel in a row of rose bushes, when an old man passing by asked how there were so many cars in the driveway of the bungalow which was in such a decrepit state. He replied to the old man that the house had been bought and the cars belonged to the owner. The old man wondered aloud why the owner needed so many cars. 'Well, perhaps he likes cars,' he told the old man, enjoying the charade. The old man was very curious and asked him if he could meet the owner. 'Yes, of course,' he replied to him. He told the old man to wait in the parlour and went into the house, ostensibly to call the owner. He changed his clothes and then stepped back out into the parlour, where the old man was waiting. When he saw him, the poor old man was confused and asked him where the owner was. 'Why, right here,' he said, pointing at himself. I laughed loudly when this story was narrated to me. "What happened after that?" I had asked. "Oh, nothing, he was served tea and then sent on his way," he replied with a smile.

"A lot of this area," Uncle continues, was wilderness. "People also warned me that there could be complications later with possession of military land. But I had already given advance payment for two other houses in the cantonment on the advice of the Inspector General of Police, who was my friend. Of course, we ended up buying this one."

"God has always helped me," he reflects. "And maybe the fact that I have never been corrupt or broken the law worked in my favour. When I wanted to extend this bungalow at the back, I did so with proper authorization. Today, this bungalow is probably the biggest in the cantonment and quite a status symbol."

"Why did you not choose either of the other two houses?" I ask. He replies, "We liked one of them quite a bit. It was owned by a retired Lieutenant General, but he had passed away not long before that and his widow met us when we went to see the house. She kept lamenting about how much she missed her husband and how unsafe she now felt there because of the miscreants in the area. Without saying anything, my wife gesticulated to me that we should leave. I instantly got up and we left. She told me later that she had felt uncomfortable listening to the widow and that the atmosphere of the house was oppressive."

When I came to know which house he was talking about, I told him, "Uncle, I am most impressed with Aunty's intuition." "Why?" he asks me. "Because I know the people who stay in the house now and I can tell you that it is not a happy house," I reply.

But honestly, what impresses me more is that a man like him would so unquestioningly obey his wife and heed her advice. And that too, at a far more patriarchal time. As if guessing what I am thinking, he says that his wife was more than just his spouse: she was also his mentor and guide. "Would you discuss your business matters with her?" I want to know. "Yes," he says, "and she was also very astute and would give very sound advice. Back in 1989, an acquaintance of ours who was a Chartered Accountant desperately wanted his son to be admitted to one of the most prestigious schools of Lucknow, Saint Francis, but all his influence had proved useless for the same. He came over to my house and asked me for my help. He said he had heard that I was very close to the Principal, a Christian Father, who had granted me the privilege of choosing a candidate for one seat in the school every year. He begged me to help him get his son admitted to the school. Before I could say anything, my wife said that it would be done, but she needed a favour in return. "Of course, bhabhiji, tell me," he said. She told him that she wanted him to register our business as a Private Limited Company. She had recently met a friend in Aminabad, who had boasted about having their own company and the perks and privileges of it and she had not been able to get it out of her mind. He said it would surely be done. I drove to the school with him that very day. The peon immediately opened the door to the Principal's office for me. I walked in and the Father dismissed the visitor in his office and asked me what the matter was. I told him that I wanted to get a child admitted to the school. Perhaps offended by the fact that I was so brazenly demanding this in front of another person, he said in a perfunctory manner that it would be done. "Not 'would be done,' Father," I said. "It has to be done right now." 'Right,' said the Father, probably realizing it was best not to cross me," he says with a smile. "The child was granted admission into the school a short while later."

"The company was named Ambalika Chit Funds Pvt. Ltd. We wanted to name it Ambika after our son, but there were already many companies with that name. Ambalika is part of the trio of the three goddesses Ambe, Ambika, and Ambalika from the Mahabharata. The name proved lucky for us and we subsequently named all of our companies Ambalika."

Coincidentally, Ambika, his son, walks into the room at that very moment and enquires whether I have tasted the coffee from their new coffee machine. "Only the black coffee, not the other fifty flavours," I answer with a smile. His father, meanwhile, tells him to get some mangoes packed for me to take home. "Please, Uncle, not 'some,' I plead," having seen the size and number of the mangoes he had sent previously, but he ignores my plea. Oh well, I think to myself, another bounty for my maids. Meanwhile, another flavor of coffee arrives for me.

"How much time did it take you to repair this house," I ask as I sip my coffee. He laughs and replies the work is still going on. Of course, he means minor ongoing repairs and refurbishments. "It was entirely my wife's effort," he says. "She would supervise everything. She oversaw all the arboriculture from the very first tree. The other day, one of my daughters informed me that several potted plants outdoors had withered; I told her that none of us can tend to the plants and gardens the way their mother did."

"I have been asked many times if the majestic trees in the gardens were already there when we bought it and I answer that each tree was planted by my wife. Everyone is amazed to learn that it was she who planned the entire landscaping from the trees to the gardens to the gazebos."

"Would you like to go now?" he asks. "You must be tired." "Oh no," I reply, "I love listening to your stories." But I think that perhaps he is tired so I decided to end the session. He tells me he will continue the story next time from when he left the SDC's house in Bareilley. "The next ten years of my life after that were probably the toughest," and I wonder what could be tougher than being beaten up constantly as a boy, having to live alone in his village, and then having to leave his home at the tender age of thirteen to a jungle far away.

RAABTA

Sandwiches are already laid out for me when I reach the house a few days later. Uncle always insists that his car will fetch and drop me, although my house is but a stone's throw from their house. Mrinalini greets me warmly and tells me that her father has not yet had his tea because he was waiting for me to join him.

"Even before I turned eighteen, I was considered 'settled' by societal standards because I had a steady job that paid me ninety rupees a month. I was also making some extra money because I would vet bills and sanction payments for Junior Engineers and they would give me a percentage of the commission they received. It was just the way it was in those days," he laughs, "not so much corruption as tradition. My expenses were not more than about twenty or thirty rupees a month, so I managed to save quite a bit of money."

"Being a clerk in those days was considered a big thing. I had moved into the house of a gentleman from my office. In those days, the state of Uttar Pradesh had three predominant castes: Kayasthas, Muslims, and Agarwals. This gentleman was from a respectable Agarwal family and had a big house, one section of which was unoccupied. This section had two bedrooms a verandah and a courtyard. He offered it to me, saying I could give him any amount I liked as rent."

"So I had a permanent government job and also my own very respectable living quarters. I started receiving offers of marriage. I was quite firm that I should have an arranged marriage decided by my family, though I did once go to see a girl on my own at someone's insistence; I remember her getting tea into the room and sitting down in front of me," he chuckles. "You went to see a girl all by yourself?" I ask, quite impressed. "Yes, I did," he replies, "although I was not comfortable with the idea of flirting with numerous proposals like a lot of other young men, though the boys in the Kayastha (Kayastha is a caste, which along with Brahmins had access to formal education in medieval India) family of the SDC with whom I had stayed and later moved out because of the sister, had been like me. They too did not believe in love affairs or flirtations."

"Somehow, news of my status reached my family in Lucknow," he goes on. I asked if he had been in touch with them ever since he left home and he replied that he had not. "It was after this that my mother, accompanied by my brother, visited me in Bareilley. It was the first time I had seen her after leaving home. I do not recall whether she came on her initiative or I asked her to visit, but I do remember that she was very happy to see what I had made of myself. She stayed with me for almost two months and it was a lovely time for us both. She would cook for me and ladle out food for me herself. When I would be in office, she would happily spend time with my landlord's family, with whom she had become quite close."

"In the meantime, I had finally decided to leave my employment and go into business for myself. One of the Junior Engineers whom I had worked with in the Sub-Division told me to come to Lucknow, where he would help me get started. I applied for a month's earned leave from my job and left for Lucknow bearing gifts for the entire family like attaché cases made from deer hide and things fashioned from bamboo: stuff which was unique to Bareilley and could not be found in Lucknow. Bareilley and Lucknow were like two separate worlds then."

The return of the prodigal son, I think to myself, eager to know what followed.

"Almost as soon as I returned home, I started getting wedding proposals which were originally meant for my elder brother. I was slightly better looking and carried myself better," he says modestly and chuckles. "After refusing the first few proposals because it was not considered proper for a younger brother to be married off before the elder, the family decided it was probably not too big a deal if I got married first."

"Strangely, though, they accepted a proposal from a poor family which had no dowry to give. I knew I would not see the girl before I got married and wondered what she was like, but was told by my brother-in-law that the person who had fixed the match had assured him that the girl was better looking than I was."

"If the same thing happened today, I would never have got married," he laughs, "but I suppose in those days it was part of the mystery and the charm of marriage. So in May 1959, we took the wedding party to Sesendi, the village of the bride. As per tradition, the groom's side would stay for four days in the bride's village. We were married off on the first day itself, but there was no question of my being able to see her. That night, after the marriage ceremony had already taken place, there was some ritual, probably Kanyadan (In the Hindu tradition, this is a significant ritual in which the parents of the bride, who is considered to be a form of Goddess Lakshmi, the deity of wealth and prosperity, give her away to the groom, who is considered an incarnation of Lord Vishnu), when her hand was placed in mine and I managed to get a brief glimpse of her face from underneath her veil, but the only thing I could discern was that her complexion was very fair."

We both laugh at the coyness of society in those days.

"There were numerous occasions in the next few days when I could have seen her face if I wanted to, but my scruples prevented me from doing so, even if she was my legally wedded wife!"

"What would happen during those four days of the wedding?" I enquire. "The wedding would take place on the first day," he tells me. "On the second day, there would be lunch, followed by a ceremony in which gifts were given to the bridegroom. At night, a big dinner would be held. The reception took place on the third day and on the fourth day, known as Chatursi, the bride and groom were given a bath together with a knot tied between them. After this ritual, they would feed each other Kheer (rice pudding)."

"Despite all these meetings between us, I was unable to see what my wife looked like. I had hoped I might be able to see her during the bathing ritual, which is performed by the Naun, the Nai's wife (The Nai or barber caste often performed duties in connection with marriage, matchmaking, and wedding celebrations. Nauns were also hairdressers, henna artists, and midwives), but I was not lucky in doing so. Many people have told me since that I was a fool to not have bribed the Nai's wife with five or ten rupees to show me my bride's face during the nuptial bath," he chuckles. "I did not even glance in her direction during the baths."

"There was another disappointment for me. I was hoping I would be given a bicycle as a wedding gift and each time we saw a new bicycle in the village, my friends would tell me that it must surely be a gift from my in-laws, but here too, I was left with an unfulfilled wish."

"When it was time for the Vidai (farewell ceremony organized by the bride's family), I did not want to take my wife home by bus, so I arranged for a taxi for us. Unlike today, when newlyweds sit together in the back of a car when departing, I sat in front and my wife sat at the back."

"What was Aunty wearing?" I can't resist asking. "She was wearing a lehenga, blouse, and odhni (dupatta)," he replies. "The odhni was semi-transparent. I was still too shy to turn around and look at her face, but I did glance in the rearview mirror and fleetingly saw her for the first time. She must have caught me looking because she immediately turned her face away."

"So did you like what you saw?" I ask with a smile. "Very much," he replies softly.

"When I was young, I had heard a song in Bareilley which I liked very much. I wrote down its lyrics somewhere. Bareilley, as I have mentioned to you, was mostly a Muslim town at that time and no soiree was complete without songs and poetry. At the moment when I saw my wife's face through her veil, I was immediately reminded of that song."

He searches for the song on his phone, but cannot find it. I ask him to narrate its lyrics if he remembers them and he looks up and says:

"Mast ankhon se masti chalakti rahe
Husn chan chan ke bahar nikalta rahe
Tum mere samne ao to iss tarah
Tum raho parde mein mujhko deedar ho
Yuhin ban than ke chilman me baitha karo
Husn chan chan ke bahar nikalta rahe"

How do I translate a lover's passion for his beloved in this song? Let me try:

"Let the intoxication keep dripping from your eyes
While your beauty keeps radiating from you
Appear in front of me in this way
That your beauty is hidden and I await its unveiling
Sit bedecked in your veils, while your beauty keeps radiating."

Listening to these lyrics, I can just imagine the awe and the longing of the young man who had just seen the face of his new bride for the very first time: the excitement, the mystery, and the joy. Where is to be found today, when love is so fleeting; if it is love at all to begin with?

"What was the highlight of your wedding, Uncle?" I ask, not wanting him to move on from those memories, which I am imagining vicariously and wistfully: when has a man ever been so entranced with just a glance at my face?

He thinks for a moment and then says that there was no Jaimala (garlanding ceremony) those days. The guy would go over to the girl's house and she would (I assume from behind many veils) shower rice and flowers on the groom. Then there would be a banquet and the wedding party would return to their lodgings. I interject to ask how many people comprised his wedding party and he replies that it was around fifty.

"At night," he says, "the Pheras would be held (In a Hindu marriage ceremony, the Pheras are the seven sacred rounds that the bride and groom take around the holy fire. Only after the bride and the groom have completed the Saat Phere are they considered husband and wife). The next day, there would be another feast and the groom would be taken to the bride's house in a palanquin."

"Did you sit in a palanquin?" I ask, quite astonished, since I have only ever seen and heard of brides being carried in palanquins. "Yes," he answers with a laugh.

"But of course, the bride would be as good as invisible!" he says, laughing louder.

Perhaps the highlight of my protagonist's wedding was the brief glimpse he had of his wife's face in the car, I muse since he has just described more details from the wedding and not shared any particularly significant moment apart from that one.

"What did Aunty wear on those four days?" I question him further, wanting to extract every little detail of the wedding. "Lehengas," he says. "She wore lehengas on numerous occasions all through her life, especially on Karvachauth (the annual ritual of fasting for the husband). Lehengas never went out of fashion, I guess; they just got more and more detailed and expensive."

"Her wedding lehenga was also expensive and she kept it with her till the end," he says quietly.

"And what did you wear to your wedding?" I ask, feeling a little intrusive now. "I wore a Jama, a long tunic," he answers.

"The most significant thing for me," he says, finally replying to my question about the highlight of his wedding, "was the realization that my bride was more beautiful than I could ever have imagined her to be. Better than all the girls I had come across till then and even better than the heroines I had seen in films." Ever her ardent fan, he reiterates that all their relatives and friends would call her Asha Parekh or Vyjanthimala.

"But you were quite popular with the fairer sex," I comment, "did you not come across anyone like Aunty?" "No," he replies without hesitation. "Many girls were indeed attracted to me, but the attraction was always one-sided. There was this incident just before I got married," he laughs, "when some of my friends persuaded me to write a love note to a pretty girl who was known to like me very much. I had also seen her looking at me interestedly many times. Well, I wrote the note to her, albeit a little reluctantly, and she wrote back immediately, saying she was from a respectable family and could never imagine a dalliance with me, so I should never again entertain the idea of it! I was not perturbed, since the attraction had been more from her side anyway, and it became a closed chapter for me. The irony of it was that when I got married, we were invited over to the girl's house because we were distantly related, and there she cornered me and asked me why I had betrayed her by getting married to someone else. When I asked her how I could have betrayed her when she was the one who had rejected me, she asked me why I had taken her first response seriously when that is what all girls from good families did. She told me she was ready to marry me even then; even willing to become my second wife! When I told her not to entertain such foolish thoughts, she said she would consume poison if I did not accept her! I explained to her that it was probably destined for us to not be together and that she should not make herself so miserable because she would soon find herself a nice guy. Thankfully, she let the matter go. Later, when she was applying Catechu (a red dye) to my wife's feet as part of a custom, I couldn't resist asking her jokingly if she was applying colour to her co-wife's feet," he chuckles.

Risky, I think to myself, but I am smiling. "Was Aunty not shocked?" I question him. "No," he says, still chuckling, "I had told her what had happened and she had laughed about it, saying at least she knew now what my choice was like, upon which I said that if that girl was ever my choice, it was only because I had not met her till then. The girl was also not offended at the co-wife comment and sportingly told my wife that she would happily choose that role if my wife permitted her to do so."

Thank God that ended well, I think, and that the girl did not end up doing something drastic, otherwise the story would have been quite different.

Just then, Mrinalini's husband, Rama Kant Pandey, the very upright bureaucrat who had hosted us in Bijnor not long ago, walks into the room to meet his father-in-law. He greets me formally, but seeing that we are in the midst of our book session, respectfully leaves the room.

"There is one incident which I will not forget till my dying day," Uncle resumes the conversation. "When we returned to Lucknow after we were married, she could not immediately move in with me because we had to wait for the auspicious time that would permit her to enter my home. Till then, she stayed at the house of the person who had fixed our marriage. I was dying to see her, now that we were married, so one morning I sneaked into the house where she was staying. I shouldn't have done so, of course," he says a little guiltily as if he had planned to meet a girlfriend and not his legally wedded wife, "but I couldn't resist."

"I was at the doorway of her bedroom when I saw her. She had just emerged from her bath because her long hair was wet. She was sitting on a chest in front of a mirror, combing out her hair. She must have sensed my presence, for she turned around and that was the moment when I saw her properly for the first time. And it was the most beautiful face I had ever seen."

My breath catches for an instant. Oh, for love like that, I think to myself and Kahlil Gibran's poem on love somehow comes to my mind:

Like sheaves of corn he gathers you unto himself.
He threshes you to make you naked.
He sifts you to free you from your husks.
He grinds you to whiteness.
He kneads you until you are pliant;
And then he assigns you to his sacred
fire, that you may become sacred bread for
God's sacred feast.
All these things shall love do unto you
that you may know the secrets of your
heart, and in that knowledge become a
fragment of Life's heart.

"She was wearing a dark green saree," he goes on, oblivious to my wistfulness, "with a thin decorative border and a blouse of the same kind. She was not wearing any makeup and she never did wear any, throughout her life. She did not need to. Seeing her, I felt like the most fortunate man ever."

"What was her reaction when she saw you?" I asked, still wistful at this hugely romantic story. "She was stricken with embarrassment," he replies, "and I immediately withdrew and left."

"Anyway," he says, moving on from what was probably the most tender moment of his life, "my elder brother also got married about a month later. We were all staying at my sister's house in Lucknow; about seven or eight of us. I was now on medical leave from my job in Bareilley, which I had taken right after my earned leave was over. Getting leave was not that big a deal at that time."

"So when did you finally return to Bareilly?" I ask. "I never returned," he chuckles. "If the first miracle of my life was that I secured permanent employment without asking for it or applying for it, the second was that I never formally resigned from my employment."

"How is that possible, Uncle?" I query him with puzzlement. He laughs and says that he went to Bareilley alone after three months of leaving, collected his pay, and left without ever tending a resignation and no one ever bothered to find out what had happened to him after that. "These days, there would be a Central Bureau of Investigation inquiry or some police inquiry at least for something like that, but even in those days, it was remarkable that no one bothered to search for a missing government employee."

We both laugh heartily at this statement.

"After I returned, my eldest brother told me to shift into the house which he had started building on a plot of land he had bought when Zamindari was abolished and my family had been granted government bonds in lieu of our land. This house was not yet complete: it had no doors or windows, the walls were not plastered and the floor was nothing but mud, but my wife and I shifted into it quite happily. We hung curtains on the open niches where the windows would eventually come."

"By then, I had started my contracting business and my first contract was for the clearing and cleaning of canals. My wife supported me completely in my decision to leave my government job, saying she knew I could easily earn far more than the ninety rupees that I was drawing as a salaried employee if I worked for myself."

"I had finally bought a bicycle (the much-coveted bicycle, I smile inwardly) and I would cycle to work and back, about a hundred and fifty kilometres a day. I would leave at six in the morning and return in the late afternoon. It was the month of June, a little over a month after my marriage. It wasn't easy cycling back and forth in the peak of summer, with the harsh loo blowing right into my face."

Before he can continue, his son walks into the room and a conversation ensues, which I try not to hear, but I still can't help hearing the words 'Chairman' and 'Resignation.' I gather that Uncle has told his son that he would like to retire from the Chairmanship of some entity, but that his son is against this decision. Suddenly, the son turns to me and asks if I think his father should retire. I am embarrassed to be included in what is a personal family matter, but since I have been asked my opinion directly, I reply with a definitive 'No.' The mental and physical faculties of the man whose biography I am writing are those of a much younger man and I cannot imagine him leading a retired, sedentary life or finding it remotely fulfilling.

When he leaves the room, his father does not address the matter with me and continues with the story, "We stayed alone in that unfinished house for about two months. My wife would spend most of her time cooking, washing, and cleaning. That was the role of wives in those days. But I marvel now at how talented and farsighted she was; I often discuss it with my children and they completely agree: shifting the children to an English medium school from a Hindi medium one, shifting into this bungalow which was a ruin and transforming it completely, getting all the daughters married to officers in the Indian Administrative Services, encouraging her daughter in law to enter politics, sending her eldest grandson to America and our daughter to Germany to study and supporting her only granddaughter's wish to study in London; where did the wife of a simple clerk get such lofty ideas from? I did not have the vision for all this."

"But you were the wind beneath her wings Uncle; you were the one who supported her in every way," I tell him, "and after all, you were the pioneer of it all," but he insists that he did not have her prescience.

I was later told another story by the family about how Aunty had handed over a little note to her grandson when he was leaving for foreign shores for the first time. The note said 'Lo himmat se kaam, badhe raho aviram, naani ma aka ashirvaad hamesha tumhare saath hai': 'Be strong, be courageous, keep on walking without stopping, your grandmother's blessings are with you.'

"Well, she did grow up in the court of a Raja," I say. "Yes, she did see the splendor and opulence of royal life while she was growing up, but neither she nor I could have imagined that one day she would live like a Queen. And I do not hesitate in saying that today we have the same status as the Raja of Sesendi, even though we were not born royal. I would venture to say that we command even more respect there than the erstwhile ruler. In the village where she grew up so poor and where even my dream of owning a bicycle did not materialize, my wife helped hundreds of girls get married. At times, she would do so all on her own, going there by herself and donating up to ten lakh rupees. She was always very charitable. She gave more than a lakh of rupees a few days before her death to the servant who just served us tea, for his sister's marriage."

I already know of Rama Aunty's magnanimity and compassion. One time, she visited the constituency of her daughter-in-law and came across a destitute young woman who had been unable to get married because her parents had no dowry to give; she put together a complete dowry for her and got her married. Even years later, she would enquire about the young woman from her daughter-in-law and ask if she was doing well. She was particularly compassionate towards young girls as is evident from the story of Priya, her young maid, who was caught stealing by a family member. She did not dismiss her as she had grown very fond of her and ignored the pleas of the family that she could not be trusted and was also insolent. Priya remained faithfully in her service for many years.

"I would have liked to meet Aunty," I say. "She would have given you a lot of love," Uncle says. "Everyone who met her was overcome by her warmth and affection."

"When I got married and started my own business," he goes on, harking back to the early days of his marriage, "my wife went to stay in her parents' village for a few days, as was the custom. I couldn't stay away from her and twice or thrice, I went off to her village to meet her without informing my family. Mind you, it wasn't so easy to travel the twenty-five kilometres to her village from the city because transport was so rudimentary. I would tell my family that I was staying at my work site. Unfortunately, my deception was discovered because my clerk came home from the site one day and asked my family where I was because I had not reported for work for three days!"

We both laugh at this story.

"Was Aunty instrumental in the family shifting here to the cantonment?" I ask. He answers that it was a joint decision between them. "Learning to make joint decisions is an important part of any long-term relationship. While decisions start small, like what should be had for dinner, they get bigger. Developing a reliable basis for decision-making and discussion provides a good foundation for a long-lasting relationship. It could be reason or logic, where you consciously draw on the facts in front of you and your previous knowledge or intuition, a 'gut feeling', where your decision has to 'feel right' to you. Intuition is a combination of your previous experience and your values, so it is a valuable tool. We did everything by consensus, relying both on reason and intuition. And if I felt very strongly about something, she would not oppose me and it was the same for me. As far as shifting to the cantonment was concerned, she was initially apprehensive, because we were well settled in such a large and comfortable home in Rajendernagar, but I explained to her that in the long term, it would be a much better option and she soon concurred with me."

"I never could have imagined that my dream of owning a bicycle would be so surpassed with me owning Land Cruisers and Mustangs today," Uncle contemplates aloud. "A poor man like me, who went to the hospital when my first child was born in a rickshaw owned by a friend!"

Yes, I think to myself, it is indeed a classic rags-to-riches story but with some very special elements thrown in.

"For me though," he continues, "it has always been more about our status and the respect that we earned through hard work and a little bit of luck. I was just a poor clerk with nothing to my name, but I became friends with the crème de la crème of society, earned the respect of those with power, status, and influence, and most importantly, became a pillar of the Brahmin community."

"My wife had shared with me the incident of the death of the Raja of Sesendi's wife and how they dressed her body in an expensive Banarsi silk saree. I never forgot the story and when she passed away, I made sure that she departed like a Queen. She was dressed in the most expensive silk saree she owned. Her final journey was in an ambulance, not a hearse, and it was decorated fully with flowers. It was followed by a cavalcade of over three hundred cars. Lucknow city traffic came to a standstill as we made our way to the cremation ground. The traffic police had instructions to stop the traffic at all roundabouts as if some VVIP was traversing the city. The Commissioner of Police was waiting for us at the cremation ground with about fifteen police cars and he helped me out of my car and escorted me down to where the pyre was to be lit."

"There were more than a thousand people at the funeral. It was in her destiny to go in style and splendor. I sometimes used to worry about how it would all transpire when she passed away because she always said she wanted to die before me: would it be in the peak heat of summer, the cold of winter, or would it be raining? But as it happened, she went in the fairest of weather."

Yes, I think to myself, on a night when the entire country was lit up with lamps and candles. Quite a way to go.

There is no silver lining to bereavement, but we all try and find comfort wherever we can. When my parents disappeared in the deluge at one of the holiest pilgrimage towns in the country, I was told by family members that the town was called Mukti Dham or the Abode of Salvation and so they would certainly have attained salvation by dying in that place. I wanted to tell Uncle that the materfamilias beloved by all departed on the most auspicious night resplendent with light, when hope and joy and prayer abounded in the hearts of all; but I knew it would be cold comfort for him to hear this just as it had been for me to hear of certain salvation for my family members. For him and his family, there would always be darkness inside their hearts on the night of Diwali even as the world rejoiced; at least until time started fossilizing the pain and they would start being grateful that she passed away with light surrounding her, her family and friends by her side, and enveloped in flowers.

"Rulers were like Gods for us," Uncle says, remembering where we had left off last time, "but the same ruler started venerating us as we venerated him at one time." He smiles and adds that when Mulayam Singh, the Chief Minister of the State, attended the wedding of his daughter and saw the Raja of Sesendi there (who was also serving as a Member of Parliament then), he was pleasantly surprised and asked him how it was that he was there. "This is my home," proclaimed the Raja, "and this is my family."

"What kind of man was Mulayam Singh?" I ask of the famous politician who dominated the politics of the state for decades. "He was a man of his word, unlike a lot of other politicians," he replies. "At one time, I needed to get my brother-in-law transferred somewhere. He honoured his word to me, although he had to turn down a man from his community to do it."

"Over the years, as we grew in power, influence, and status, we became the Raja's peers and then friends, although there was always a bit of rancor from their side because unlike them, we came from nothing."

"By 1990, my status equaled the Raja's. His progeny had not been able to hold on to their wealth and status. They were staying in Sesendi House, their royal residence, which was far smaller than my three-and-a-half-acre bungalow. The Raja requested me to intervene with them on his behalf on several occasions and guide them in business. When I met them, they would smoke in front of me and I told them that if they wanted to achieve anything in life, they should first start respecting their elders."

"But there was always this simmering discontent between us, which came to the fore during an incident when my mother-in-law got a field harvested in Sesendi which the Raja claimed was his. In retaliation, the

Raja's brother had one of his henchmen fire at one of our buses, which caused the driver to be quite seriously injured. I had previously helped the Raja out in a murder case of a Member of the Legislature in which he had been framed. I filed a case against his brother who shot my driver and went to the Raja to tell him this. "It's a fraudulent case you have filed," said the Raja, "what harm can it do to us?" I told him that he had not been so nonchalant when a false charge had been filed against him in the murder case. The Circle Officer was with me when I said this; he had come along to try and persuade the Raja to rein in his brother. The Raja was very miffed with this. He told the Director General of Police, who was related to him, to transfer the Circle Officer out of the city that very night."

"I then arranged for a police raid to be carried out on the Raja's property to locate the perpetrator of the crime. Seeing that things were getting out of hand, the Raja decided to call a truce and in the morning, I was asked to come over to work out a compromise. The Raja's son confronted me when I reached their house and asked me how I could have had the nerve to get a raid carried out against people of their status. The policeman who was with me reminded him that I was the one who had helped them in the murder case. The Raja acknowledged that my help had been invaluable, but told me that what I had done was wrong nevertheless and that it had lowered his dignity in the eyes of his people."

"Meanwhile, the brother of the driver who had been injured also decided to take revenge and shot the Raja's henchman who had fired at his brother. The henchman received a bullet in his foot. In the hospital, however, this henchman suddenly required a blood transfusion for some reason, which caused a severe reaction in his body, killing him. Suddenly, the news spread that it was me who had the henchman killed in the hospital." He laughs as he says this and adds that sometimes false rumours help in enhancing a man's reputation!

"Everyone started believing that I was way more powerful than the Raja, as I had a raid conducted at his house while he stood helplessly by and because I was assumed to have had his man killed."

"My goodness," I laugh. "That's quite a story!"

"Oh, there are too many such stories," he comments.

"But let me not undermine the influence of the Raja in my life. It was because we aspired to a life like theirs that my wife and I worked so hard towards our success. And overall, we remained quite cordial with each other. The Raja's sisters used to visit my wife often. It was one of the Raja's sisters and her husband who took my wife to the hospital when she had her Tetanus attack."

"Would it be okay to use the real names of the people in your book?" I want to know, thinking it might not be proper or advisable to do so. "Of course, why not," he replies nonchalantly.

"Well, coming back to the story, after more than a year of us having been in Lucknow with my family, during which I was undertaking contracting work and had just about managed to graduate to a motorcycle, problems started brewing between my brothers and me, especially my eldest brother. We were now all staying together in the house to which my eldest brother had sent my wife and me, and the construction of which I had completed myself. I even had two more rooms constructed at the back with the money from my contracting business."

"Were you more successful than your brother?" I enquire, thinking that jealousy may have rekindled the long-standing friction between his eldest brother and him. "No," he replies, "he was a clerk and receiving about the same salary as I was."

"Then was it the women who created tensions within the family?"

"No," he answers once again, "the women got along pretty well and they did the housework according to a roster of duties. My wife in any case was very adjusting and amiable."

"Then what was the problem?" I want to know.

Thinking a bit, he says that perhaps it was the fact that his wife's parents would visit them often and with gifts of farm produce and this might have made the others jealous. The parents of the other two daughters-in-law never visited. One's parents lived too far away and the others were far too poor.

He pauses in the conversation and insists that I have something more to eat and I plead that I really cannot eat anymore and that I also need to watch my weight, at which he scoffs with a smile. Seeing that I am unrelenting, he carries on with the narrative.

"It had been almost two years in that house when my mother contracted cancer." "Cancer of what?" I interject. "Of the uterus," he says. "In the olden days, there was no cure for cancer and in any case, we did not have the money for any fancy treatment. We did take her to Patna once on the advice of someone, but she was running a fever at the time and we were told that nothing could be done till the fever went away. We did not have any medicines for fever even then, so we came back to Lucknow."

His granddaughter Nandaja breezes into the room and says a cheery Hi to me. "Have you eaten anything?" she asks immediately and I almost laugh out loud. The entire family must think I am malnourished, I think to myself. "Yes, I have already had kebabs and sandwiches, thank you," I answer.

She looks at the aquarium in the corner of the room where we are sitting: the covered verandah overlooking the gardens with the gazebos, and asks her grandfather if it can be shifted to the office. Her grandfather acquiesces immediately. She smiles and waves goodbye to us.

"The tension in the family had escalated by then. We had become parents to a baby girl and for a few months, I sent my wife to her village so that she and the baby would be spared the tension in the house and be well looked after. I moved temporarily to Fatehpur near Barabanki because I had secured a contract to supervise the building of a canal there. We would all contribute twenty-five rupees to the running of the house each month, but since my wife and I were both away for a few months, I felt that I did not need to pay towards the expenses for that duration. I do not know whether I was justified in this but at any rate, when I returned, my eldest brother demanded my share of the money. I refused. My relationship with him was already precarious. When my daughter was born, he took a rickshaw to the hospital to see her but demanded that I pay the three or four annas for the ride. There was not much sibling love left between us if there ever had been. I remember that even immediately after the birth of my daughter, my wife would have to wash utensils at night with freezing cold water, after which she would light a few coals to warm her hands."

"When my mother passed away, things deteriorated further. My brother moved us out to a small garret on top of the garage. My wife and I were still quite content with our own little space and being able to do our cooking, but my brother resented this as well. He started locking the door at the entrance of the house which led to the toilet at night, so that we were unable to use it all night. When this provoked no reaction from us, he ordered me to vacate the house, saying I had no claim to it; even though it had been purchased with family money and I had finished its construction with my money. Before I could react, he started pushing me towards the door. My wife's brothers tried to intervene, but my wife stopped them, saying they should not intervene in family matters. On the other hand, his brothers-in-law, who were also staying in the house at the time, manhandled my wife's brothers. My sister's father-in-law was also present in the house and told my brother that he had no right to treat me that way, but he was told to mind his own business. There was nothing we could do and so on that cold January evening, we were thrown out of the house and into the street. My brother did not even care for our ten-month-old daughter: he led her out into the cold. The door of the house was locked behind us. We stood there on the road with our meager possessions: a cot, a box, and two pitchers which had been a wedding present, and with nowhere to go."

"My sister's house was in the same neighbourhood and she had two spare rooms in her house. I asked her if we could rent them from her but she refused, saying that she could not cross my eldest brother. I wondered where to take my family. Meanwhile, our infant daughter needed to use the toilet. We had no choice but to make her squat on the road. Fortunately for us, a kindly neighbour who had witnessed our plight came to our rescue by getting us a mug of water so we could wash her. A possible reason for my brother's intense dislike of us," he says as if it has suddenly dawned on him, "could have been that all our neighbours were very fond of us, especially of my wife."

"We might have spent the whole night freezing on the sidewalk, but the person who had arranged our marriage landed up there on his bicycle. He used to stay close by and had probably learned what had transpired. He called for a rickshaw, helped us load our possessions in it, and took us to his home, saying that he had enough room in his house for us. He put us up in a section of the house that had two bedrooms, a courtyard, and a kitchen. He had another few empty rooms at the back, which an engineer friend of mine later rented from him when he was posted to Lucknow."

Digressing from that harrowing night, he laughs and says that the engineer friend was quite a character: he had his wife and children in the village, but had secretly got married a second time to a girl from Shahjahanpur, where he used to go to teach tuition!

"I felt like I had met God Himself that night," he says of the man who took them home that day. "He gave us warm milk for our daughter, fed us a hot meal, and told us that after breakfast together the next morning, we could go and buy whatever kitchen essentials we required to start our kitchen."

"For two people who had been staying with their baby girl in what was nothing more than an attic to have two spacious rooms with a toilet, a kitchen, and even a courtyard, was luxury. Things started looking up for us from then on. I secured a contract for cutting down trees to build a canal and I sold the trees, which happened to be Indian Rosewood, for a handsome profit of more than ten thousand rupees. It was a windfall for us."

"A few days later, as I was cycling back home, I saw that a vacant plot very close to my brother's house was being auctioned off. Without even thinking, perhaps led by the perverse pleasure of owning property where he would see it every day. I bid seven thousand rupees for the plot," he chuckles.

Mrinalini breezes into the room with the cheeriest of Hellos and asks me, as usual, if I have had anything to eat or drink. I laugh and tell her I have, but her father still orders a black coffee for me, saying I must be tired. Tired? I have been so engrossed in the story that I have almost lost track of time.

"We bought new furniture, clothes, and other household things that we had not been able to afford before that with the money that I made from the sale of the Rosewood trees. In the meantime, I also won the suit that I had filed against my brother for my share in the family house. I might not have taken the matter to court if my brother had not taunted me when he evicted us that I would not get a share in the house even if I fought for it and the man who so kindly sheltered us had not advised me to seek recourse in the law instead of getting into any kind of altercation with my brother. The court granted me one-fourth share of our family house. My brothers were shocked and they conspired to sweet talk me into taking the portion of land behind the house which had a very narrow lane in front of it. They told me that since I was now a rich man who had my property, I could afford to be magnanimous. I relented because money had never been the driving force in my life anyway."

"Once again, perhaps because I had forfeited what was rightfully mine without any rancour, fortune favoured me. The narrow lane in front of my portion of the house was widened into a fifty-foot wide road by the government," he laughs. "My brothers were left with their fifteen-foot sections, while mine grew to forty-five feet!"

"There was an old sanyasi (Hindu religious mendicant) who came over to the family house before we were evicted. For no reason at all, he handed me a fish made of silver and a coin and told me to keep them safely forever. He also said that I would never forget him. Maybe the silver fish and coin were the talismans that kept us from ruin. I searched for him for a long time, but never found him."

"Anyway, I built two rooms in my section of the family home and put them out on rent for forty rupees a month. We continued staying with the man who had rescued us on that cold winter night. My wife opened a separate bank account for the rent money, saying that we would save it to perform a Gaya Pind Daan for our family (the Gaya Pind Daan is performed by Hindus in Gaya in Bihar so that the departed souls of their ancestors can attain peace and salvation)."

"The ceremony is performed by the youngest male member of the family. My youngest brother had passed away a few years earlier, so my wife insisted that his elder son should perform the ritual. We all were on fairly good terms by then. When the sons returned from Gaya after performing the ceremony, I informed them that I was giving them my section of the house with the two rooms I had built on it. However, I heard them talking amongst themselves, expressing doubt about me giving them the property. I immediately bought stamp papers worth seventy-five thousand rupees and registered the property in their name that very day. After that, I handed them another five hundred rupees and told them to buy sweets to commemorate the occasion."

I almost shake my head in disbelief. Being evicted twice from his house by his eldest brother but still reconciling with him and even acceding to his family's unfair terms, bequeathing his portion of the house to his late brother's sons, raising his wife's three younger brothers like his own, giving away forty bighas (in Uttar Pradesh state, a bigha can vary from 0.2 to 0.6 acres) of land to his in-laws which his wife and he had bought early on under the Patta system, (Patta is a type of land deed issued by the government to an individual for a small piece of land with a land revenue exemption: the cess was then twenty percent of the revenue) and handing over his four-acre farm in the village to them as well simply because they had started living there on the pretext that their house on the Raja's land was infested with snakes: is the hero of this book even real? When I had learned earlier about the forty bighas of land and the four-acre farm, I had asked him why he had given away the land to his in-laws just because they had started living there, he simply replied that he could not possibly have asked them to move out.

"My wife believed in saving money more than spending it," he says, and I am reminded of how much charity she did with all the money she saved up. "Neither of us were spendthrifts. We lived and ate well, but we were not into flaunting our wealth or spending on luxuries like fine dining. We believed in building assets. Of course, we did splurge on our children's weddings. We spent about eighty lakhs on my son's wedding in 2000," he says, without any trace of arrogance. I can't help commenting on how large a sum of money that was in those days. "Yes, and in 2005, we spent about seventy lakhs on my youngest daughter's wedding," he adds matter-of-factly.

"When I started my contracting business, only ten or twelve trucks were operating in Lucknow and we were at their mercy, always waiting for them to show up. I realized it would be easier and profitable for me to buy my own truck. With the help of a middleman, I bought a second-hand truck for nine thousand rupees, paying six thousand rupees in cash and taking out a loan for the rest."

"Unfortunately, the truck I bought was not very roadworthy. I was tricked by the middleman. It was always breaking down and I incurred a lot of expenditure on it. The first time it broke down, my wife told me to mortgage her gold necklace to get it repaired. The second time, its engine had seized and I did not have the money to replace it. She went by herself to a jeweler and mortgaged all her jewellery except for a nose pin and a pair of earrings. She returned and handed me the money. I was appalled that she had mortgaged her jewellery and didn't want to take the money, but I had no choice. If that wasn't bad enough, I could never pay off the mortgage and get back her jewellery. I had thought that owning a truck meant I could stop my contracting business because even owners of single trucks were very rich men those days, but I had not catered for all the breakdowns and constant repairs. We had to sell all her jewellery. My wife refused to let me be despondent, assuring me that it was only a temporary setback and that she was certain we would buy a lot of jewellery later when things got better for us."

"It was around that time that I came to be associated with Chandra Bhanu Gupta, who was the Chief Minister of Uttar Pradesh (C.B. Gupta served as the Chief Minister of the state for three terms). One of his security officers had become my friend and one day, he took me over to the Chief Minister's residence. In those days, the Chief Ministers did not have the kind of security like they do today. They also would not be ensconced inside fortress-like homes with large throngs of people waiting outside to meet them. Things were far more casual. Well, we were sitting outside the house when Guptaji emerged from inside. I must have caught his eye because he enquired who I was. I immediately rose when he approached and touched his feet. He just nodded at me without saying anything and went back in, which was understood to be his unspoken assent for my presence there. From then on, I was over at his residence almost every day," he chuckles.

"I started getting close to him because I was always hanging around the house, ready to assist wherever I could; from helping him to buy and inspect groceries to vetting his visitors. He started relying on me, instructing me from time to time to check what was happening in and around the house. I would even follow him into the kitchen whenever he went in there looking for something to eat!"

It is indeed surprising that a mere truck owner could be so close to such a high-ranking politician, even if things were different those days. It must have been his charisma that drew the Chief Minister to him, but of course the Chief Minister must also have been a humble man to encourage the close association.

"How old were you then, Uncle?" I enquire. He thinks for a second and then says he must have been about twenty-four years old because he had already had his second daughter by then.

I can't help asking him how he felt about begetting two daughters, considering that even today sons are far more coveted in Indian society. "I was perfectly happy to have daughters," he answers, "but it bothered my wife, especially since a boy was born to us after our first daughter. Unfortunately, he was premature and placed in the incubator and my mother-in-law, knowing nothing about incubators, took him out of it. He died and we buried him. My wife was inconsolable. She conceived again soon after, but another daughter was born to us. This was in 1963, when I still had only one rickety truck and our income was so low that I had to ask my friend the rickshaw puller to take me to the hospital when my second daughter was born. That night, I slept in the same rickshaw outside the hospital. It is ironic that a girl, born in such poverty, went on to get married to a high-ranking government official and never knew penury in her life."

"By then, I had built a three-room house on the plot of land I had bought at the auction, but we continued to stay in the house of the kindly gentleman who had rescued us. Eventually, when we did shift there, we had two more rooms on top and rented out the ground floor to a Montessori school. The toilet and the bathroom were still on the ground floor and we had to descend a ladder to get to them. The school fetched us a rent of four hundred rupees a month, which helped greatly with our expenses. We were still poor, but we were never ashamed of how we lived. Once, we were visited by a relative who was a Judge and he too had to climb down the ladder to access the toilet," he laughs at the memory.

"Anyway, because of my association with the Chief Minister, I was appointed President of the Uttar Pradesh Taxi Mahasangh, the Taxi Association. A lot was chosen for the Taxi Stand near the bus stand by one of Guptaji's men and the taxis started plying from Lucknow to Kanpur. Later more routes were added, such as Lucknow to Bahraich and Faizabad."

"Had you stopped the trucking business?" I ask. "No," he says, "The truck was still plying, except I had bought a new one to replace the one I had before. I now also owned a taxi, which I often drove myself. I also drove other taxis when they were supposed to be off-duty, to earn extra money. One night, I drove to Kanpur for 'Dulha utari' (dropping off the groom) and earned five rupees as a tip. Every rupee counted for me," he says with a smile.

"Did you also drive the truck?" I ask curiously. "Oh yes, very often," he replies. "On long journeys, the driver could not manage alone and I would go along and take turns driving."

"So what was the longest journey you undertook?" I ask him. "It was from Etawah to Jaunpur, a distance of about five hundred kilometres," he replies. "But there was hardly any traffic then and at the most, one would cross a truck or two. Also, for long journeys, we would usually start at night and arrive in the morning."

"And how long did you continue to drive your truck?" I ask, quite intrigued at the incongruousness of it all: a young (and very handsome) B. C. Mishra driving both trucks and taxis and spending the rest of the time with the Chief Minister of the state. "About two years," he answers.

"The taxi association soon had about a hundred taxis. I managed to buy a second truck. Most government officials in those days did not have official vehicles allotted to them and so there was a constant demand for taxis. Since I was heading the association, this ensured that I came into contact with many important people. I would provide them and their families with reliable taxis and safe drivers. The Senior Superintendent of Police of Lucknow at the time, Mr. Kaul, would request me all the time for a taxi to drive his sister-in-law and her daughter safely from Lucknow to Kanpur, where his brother was posted as the Director of Industries. I became quite close to him because of this, as with many others."

"Being the President of the Taxi Association and someone so close to the Chief Minister helped me greatly to attain success and wealth. I was getting a percentage of the token money collected by the taxis, which added up to a good amount. I also got acquainted with a whole gamut of top-ranking officials and politicians. And somehow I also became a de facto mafia head because I came in contact with many gangsters and criminals; although I was not into any kind of crime myself."

"In Lucknow?" I ask. "All over Uttar Pradesh," he answers.

JHANKAAR

I landed up on time for our next meeting and a servant led me into the bedroom of the master of the house. When I stepped into the room, however, I saw that he was not alone. His son, two daughters, and granddaughter were sitting in the room. The atmosphere was very solemn and no one said a word. I wondered what was going on and assumed that they had been discussing some personal matter. Not wanting to intrude, I asked if I should come back later or the next day. The son stood up and told me to stay; explaining that they had just come across their mother's will and had been overwhelmed by it. It was then that I noticed the tears in the eyes of his sisters and daughter, who also stood up to excuse themselves from the room.

Oh gosh, I think to myself, embarrassed to have witnessed such a delicate moment, but wanting to express empathy by telling the father and son that it was going to hurt for a long, long time and that there would be many more such painful moments, like when they all finally gathered the courage to go through her things and have to touch each of her personal effects. And that it would hurt even more to have to give some of them away.

I want to say that each time they come across an object that has her memory associated with it, they will cry. That places and songs and smells will sear their hearts for years.

I want to say that they will miss her each time the family is together for a special occasion and that they will feel as if their hearts are breaking when her grandchildren get married and she is not there to bless them.

And I want to give myself comfort too by sharing that I have experienced all this. I remember coming across a scrap of paper with my father's scribbles on it many months after they disappeared and accidentally switching off the refrigerator in their house a few weeks after their disappearance, ruining all that was left of my mother's cooking in it: her preserves and chutneys; which she would never be making again. Those careless scribbles had been more precious to me than any literary work and the realization that I would never again be able to taste anything that my mother made had caused a meltdown.

But I stand transfixed in the room and say nothing.

Uncle finally stands up and leads me into the covered verandah. Before we can sit, Mrinalini returns with a tear-streaked face and apologizes for the scene I have just witnessed. "Mummy's will made us all very emotional," she says.

"I understand," I tell her.

"We can't get over what she has written; we did not know she could write so beautifully," she says crestfallenly, as I wonder what her mother had written in the will.

When Mrinalini and her brother had left, Uncle and I sat silently in the verandah for a while. Despite his outward demeanor of calmness, I wondered if he was composed enough to proceed with the book today and I was about to ask him when he suddenly recommenced with his story.

"I have a very dear friend in Bombay whose life has been very similar to mine. That is how we got close. We met for the first time at my grandson's engagement party in Nasik. I was helping myself to some food and he was doing the same. Our eyes met and there was an instant liking. We introduced ourselves and almost immediately realized why we had been drawn to each other. He told me he was a self-made man who had run away from home at the age of eleven and I told him I was only a little older than him when I had done the same."

"Well, then," exclaimed my friend, "let us find a place to sit and exchange our stories!"

"This friend of mine, Kumar Bihari, is originally from Siwan in Bihar," he tells me. "Like me, he started small, working for some company, and got lucky when the British left India and he managed to get the ownership of a factory. Today, he has a magnificent 10,000-square-foot house in Bombay, a forty-acre farm on the outskirts of Bombay, and several companies. He has two sons in law, one is in the Indian Administrative Service and the other is in the Indian Police Service. He also has two daughters. That's also quite a similarity, with my three sons-in-law in the Civil Services. Of course, I am also very closely associated with politics since my daughter-in-law and her father are politicians."

"Our friendship was cemented when Kumar Bihari visited Lucknow for the first time. He had lent money to an individual from Lucknow, who had told him that he would invest it for him in a property here, but had not handed over any papers to him. He wanted to try and get his money back. My driver and the official security guard assigned to me by the state government picked him up from the airport in my Mercedes car. He wondered how and why I had been given special state protection and asked them about it. What he didn't know is that ever since Mayawati became Chief Minister of Uttar Pradesh, I have always had an official gunman. Anyway, I arranged for the property to be transferred to my friend's name immediately and also paid the twenty-five lakh rupees towards stamp duty because my friend could not access such a large sum of money in such a short time."

"My friend was all agape when I paid for the registry. We had met only that one time in Nasik and he could not believe that someone would be willing to risk such a large sum of money for someone he had met just once. Till today, he compliments me for having the ability to discern who was trustworthy and who was not."

"You bought me that day with your confidence in me, he says, and I joke with him that I have never been in the business of buying and selling."

"A few days ago, a man landed up at my place with ten lakh rupees. They were owed to my friend in Bombay, and he had told the person who owed him to give me the money and that he would collect it from me later. That is the kind of friendship and trust that we share. Similarly, when my son needed to pay someone in Bombay the sum of a few lakhs and asked me if I could ask my friend to help, I told him to call my friend himself, because I was certain that he would never refuse."

"I took him on a tour of our college when he was here. He was impressed with the facilities and the fact that it is one of the twenty-eight colleges in the state out of a total of seven hundred and forty-six, which is accredited by the NBA (National Board of Accreditation). After seeing all the main facilities, he wanted to visit the boys' hostel and walked over there alone to meet the students. He enquired from them what they thought of the college and the hostel. They told him that the college had a high standard of academics and the hostel felt like home, except that the food here was better than what they got at home. My friend came back and told me that he was now truly convinced that I had set up a noteworthy educational education."

"My vision for the college students has always been that they should not strive simply for good employment; they should strive to become employers themselves and this is the spirit of entrepreneurship that I always try to inculcate in the students whenever I visit."

He halts and calls out to his servant to order spiced fritters for me, even though I plead with him that I will not be able to eat them.

"You will like them," he says, "they are special."

"What is your favourite food, Uncle?" I ask him.

"I do not have any favourite food," he replies. "I never had the time to think about food. There have been times when my wife and I ate only chapattis with palak (spinach) because it was the cheapest and the healthiest thing available. My wife and I ate to live; never lived to eat. We did not have enough money for any indulgence for most of our lives anyway."

"What about when you came into a lot of money?" I ask.

"Then we got busy making more money," he laughs.

"Was Aunty fond of jewellery?" I enquire, as we sip the black coffee that has arrived for us.

"Yes, she was very fond of buying it; once we had the money to buy it, of course. But she never really wore any of it. I always loved her buying jewellery because I could never forget how she had pawned away the little jewellery she had when I was in a financial crisis. There were only four things she wore all the time: a diamond nose pin, four diamond bangles, a gold chain with a locket, and her diamond studs. But recently, when she was in the hospital, she took off the gold chain and handed it to our youngest daughter as a birthday present."

"She was as fond of gifting jewellery as she was of buying it. She would buy lots of gold trinkets and give them away as presents on numerous occasions. A couple of days after she had passed away, one of our servant boys came to us weeping, saying that 'didi' had promised him five lakhs in cash as well as jewellery and household stuff for his daughter's wedding. Mrinalini told me that her mother had mentioned something about the jewellery to her, but she did not know about the cash amount. However, we honoured her word and gave the servant whatever he said she had promised."

"She was also fond of buying beautiful and expensive sarees from all over," he reminisces, "not only for herself but for her daughters and daughter-in-law. I do not think any of them has ever bought a saree for themselves."

"She used to sit right here with the tradespeople," he says, gesticulating with his hand around the verandah in which we are sitting. "There would always be some or the other jeweler or garment seller here."

I look around as if I expect to see the spectacle before me and have a vision of the beautiful, charitable lady amongst the sellers, examining the merchandise and buying a lot of it only to give away.

"My children and grandchildren miss her very much," he says softly. "They tell me that they now marvel at how she managed everything in the household single-handedly."

"She always dreamed big," he says, still so very much in love with his wife. "That is why we were able to achieve all that we did: the money, the status, and the power. I have told you about Sesendi village and how much respect and influence we have there. The other day, someone from the village was over and he said that people there think that B. C. Mishra is the Raja of Sesendi. People seek my blessings for the local elections there. Recently, the man who won from there asked me to preside over his inaugural speech, but I refused, saying that I had always stayed away from such stuff. I may have wielded political influence, but never wanted to get involved in it myself."

The true Kingmaker, I think to myself.

"I have still not opened her cupboards and I am not going to," he says, touching upon the old sensitive topic. "I never even pried into her stuff, except one time when I wanted to tease her about hiding stuff from me, which backfired on me. She had gone to Aminabad for shopping and I opened her cupboard, which is next to mine in the closet. I grabbed a box placed on one of the shelves to see what was in there. But as soon as I reached into the box, I let out a yell. The box contained a sharp knife and cut my hand pretty badly!"

"Knife!" I exclaim, horrified at the thought of Aunty hoarding dangerous weapons.

"Yes," he laughs seeing the expression on my face, "it was a family heirloom I had forgotten about and she had probably placed it for safekeeping inside that box. When she returned and I told her what had happened, she laughed and said it served me right for going through her things."

"My wife also never touched my money and would always ask me to hand it to her, although she and I were equal partners in our business."

"I never again went through her belongings. I believe there is a box somewhere that contains the letters we exchanged between 1959 and 1960, but I have not seen or searched for it. She would take them out every once in a while to read them. I told her once to get rid of the letters, saying our children would laugh and tease us if they came across them, but she could not bear to do so. My daughter Mrinalini told me recently that she had wrapped up the letters in a silken cloth before stowing them in the box."

She was right not to throw them away, I think. Some things deserve to be cherished and preserved. I threw my love letters and diaries into a winter bonfire a few years ago. I had just dealt with the untimely death of my parents and I did not want to leave any personal artifacts behind for my children to deal with. Plus, I sensed long before I knew it that the love that the letters harked to had become jaded; if it ever was that. Bereavement makes one want to set one's own house in order, just in case. I even sat down with stacks of family photographs taken over the years and tore up most of them, keeping only those of the children and ones that were worth keeping. When my daughter got to know what I had done, she cried and told me that it was not for me to decide what was worth keeping and what was not, because those photographs were memories for them as well."

"My birthday falls on November 3rd," Uncle breaks my chain of thought. "On my last birthday, we had the customary lunch for family and close friends and she kept sitting with our guests till late. She came inside around ten at night and told me she had ordered food for everyone from the Hotel Taj for dinner, as it was her birthday the next day. She asked me what I would like to eat, knowing that I preferred home food." I am amazed to learn that the husband and wife, whom I have come to consider true soul mates, also had their birthdays a day apart. 'What would you like to eat?' I asked her in turn and she said she wanted to eat Tehri (a simple dish made with rice, lentils, and vegetables). I said I would have the same. Fifteen minutes later, while sitting up in bed, she collapsed."

"We rushed her to the hospital that night and she never returned."

It is shocking for me to learn that Aunty was taken to the hospital on the night of her husband's birthday and the eve of hers.

"I always believed in astrology. My wife cheated death four times in her life but this time, when she was being taken to the hospital, I knew she would not return. I only told our family doctor to ensure that she would not suffer any pain."

"In 2014, I also almost died; actually, I was clinically dead for twenty minutes. I had suffered a bout of bronchopneumonia and been admitted to the hospital, but I insisted on being discharged early even though I had not recovered completely. Once back home, I developed Septicemia and my oxygen levels started dropping. I became unconscious and can only recall my wife urging everyone to airlift me to Medanta Hospital in Delhi immediately. Then, suddenly regaining consciousness, I stood up and walked by myself to the car waiting to take me to the hospital. In the car, I passed out once again and was not breathing for twenty minutes: the time it took to reach Sahara Hospital amidst a convoy of cars through dense fog. The Director of the Hospital was waiting for us outside the hospital with a bi-pap machine and a stretcher. They managed to revive me and I regained consciousness at four o'clock in the morning. I know I willed myself to come back to life so that my wife would not be left alone. She also had unshakeable faith that I could not go before her; that she would never be a widow."

"I was in hospital for a month and she spent all that time praying and telling everyone that she was certain I would return because it was in her destiny to go before me. It must have been a very tough time for her. At the time that I was rushed to hospital, our daughter Meenakshi was admitted to the ICU of the same hospital, a few floors below mine. She was in the last stages of cancer. We had tried everything to save her, including sending her to New York for treatment, but we could not. She passed away while I was in the hospital. As with my wife, I was unable to bid goodbye to her."

"How did Aunty cheat death four times?" I ask, very pained at the tragic story I had just heard, especially since I had been told that Aunty never really recovered from the loss of her young daughter.

"In 1974, she contracted Tetanus," he answers, "Something that almost no one recovered from in those days. She must have got it from the Tetanus ward where she went to visit her maid's son without telling anyone. She had a wound on her foot at the time. When I returned home from the office, I discovered she had a high fever. Fortunately, I knew the heads of department of many medical colleges and hospitals and in fact, the wife of one of them was already by her bedside when I reached and they were waiting for her husband, who had been summoned to the house. The husband was a leading doctor and upon discovering that she was unable to open her mouth, he told us to take her immediately to the hospital. On the way and also in the hospital, she had seizures, but survived nonetheless."

"The second time, she collapsed at home because of a fall. Her nerves, the doctors told us, had been weakened by Tetanus and she would often suffer falls because of it. I was at home at the time. Her eyes rolled back into her head before we knew what was happening and she had to be rushed to the hospital once again."

"The third time, she took a very heavy dose of insulin on the advice of a new doctor in a renowned hospital and it caused her to slip into a coma. Thinking initially that it was Angina, we quickly gave her a Sorbitrate tablet, but it had no effect. Then, remembering that she had taken some medicine for her blood sugar, I forced a spoonful of sugared water into her clenched mouth. Her eyelids fluttered slightly. We kept giving her sugared water till she came around."

"Also, in 1995 or 1996, she had severe chest pains and had to go for an angiography. We suspected that she had had a heart attack, but thankfully, she came back from the hospital without any complications."

"I sometimes blame myself for her death," he continues. "Two months ago, she emerged from the toilet and told me that her pain was getting unbearable. She had had surgery for a kidney problem three years ago and after that a knee replacement surgery, which would cause her Creatinine levels to shoot up. She was always in pain. Seeing her in such acute discomfort that night, I prayed for her to be delivered of her pain. And two months later, God answered my prayer."

"She was in hospital for ten days. She was put on the ventilator on the last day but was still conscious and aware. Pramod (his daughter-in-law's father) was with her when she breathed her last. He told me she passed away peacefully."

The silence hangs heavy for a while in the room. Then, to divert his attention from the painful saga, I asked him to continue the story from the time he was still President of the Taxi association and had bought his second truck.

"In 1967 Chaudhry Charan Singh defected from the Chief Minister, C. B. Gupta, along with thirty-five members of legislature, and formed his government," he says. "It was an unprecedented time. Till then, defections were unheard of, and political loyalties were paramount. Following this, defections started happening all over the country, like Morarji Desai's from Indira Gandhi. On Lal Bahadur Shastri's (the second Prime Minister of India) sudden death in January 1966, Indira Gandhi became the Prime Minister. Lal Bahadur Shastri's body was brought to India from Tashkent by Soviet Premier Kosigyn (I am getting quite a mini history lesson here). However, Indira's leadership came under challenge from Morarji Desai, who had been a close contender for the post of Prime Minister along with Indira Gandhi after Shastri's death. He was later made Finance Minister, but in 1969, he resigned to become chairman of the opposition to Indira Gandhi and the Congress Party."

Indira Gandhi: that formidable woman, a paragon in the male-dominated society of the twentieth century. There will always be conflicting political views about her leadership, but there is no denying that people of my generation grew up perceiving her as one of the greatest politicians of all time.

There is a photograph of Aunty garlanding Indira Gandhi in the gallery outside Uncle's room. I ask Uncle about it and he tells me that she met Indira Gandhi sometime in 1978 or 1979, when she visited Lucknow as Prime Minister.

"My wife was a huge fan of hers and took a friend along with her to the airport to meet her."

"Were you close to her as well, Uncle?" I ask, knowing how politically well-connected he had become over the years.

"Not close, no," he answers, "but I knew some people with a lot of clouts from her constituency, Rae Bareilley. There was an incident when a relative of mine, an RSS man (the RSS has always represented Indic values, especially Hinduism, and challenged the hegemony of the Gandhi family), was imprisoned in Moradabad jail. I called up someone I knew in Rae Bareilley in the evening and said that I wanted my man released. Those days, there was no direct calling: trunk calls had to be booked beforehand. By night, I received a call back telling me that an order for release had been issued from the Prime Minister's house and that I could send someone to Moradabad jail in the morning to pick up my man."

"Indira Gandhi took special care of the people in her constituency and no one could question or challenge the authority of any official from there. And since I was very close to some of them, there existed a kind of de facto association between her and me. There was this one incident when she was travelling by car to Rae Bareilley and our cars drew up together at a closed railway crossing. She got out of her car and came and met us. Of course, as I have said, those days the security around politicians was not what it is today."

Still! I think to myself, quite overawed.

"Having influence in Rae Bareilley helped me in many situations, although I never begged anyone for favours or bribed anyone. There is an interesting story from our Rajendarnagar days. There was a dhobi (washer man) in our locality, who was quite a goon. His wife, who was quite pretty, was his accomplice and would charm the local policemen, who spent a lot of their time with her at the shop of the dhobi. This helped him get away with a lot of petty crime."

"My wife had sort of adopted a stray calf in the colony, who she had named Somu. Somu used to follow her home like a pet dog and she would feed him and talk to him lovingly like a child. One day, we learned that Somu had been blinded and killed by the dhobi because he had chewed up some of the dhobi's clothes. The truth is, the dhobi was resentful of my influence in the area and probably killed the calf because my wife loved it so much."

"My wife was distraught over the loss of Somu. A day or two later, while she was cutting vegetables on the porch of our house, an Inspector from the police station in Rae Bareilley came to visit me. He had become my friend because I had arranged financing for him to buy a few tractors and also helped a relative of his to get a coveted contract. Upon seeing her visibly upset, he asked her what the matter was. When she told him about Somu and the dhobi, he promised her retribution for Somu's death."

"Soon after, we heard that the dhobi had been arrested on a murder charge and taken away to Rae Bareilley. The dhobi's wife guessed what must have happened and came begging to my wife to get her husband back. My wife told her that she would do so if both of them left the city immediately after his return and were never seen in the locality again. The dhobi's wife agreed and closed down their shop. Miraculously, an alibi was discovered which exonerated the dhobi and he was released from Rae Bareilley. We never saw them again."

"Around this time, I also had an incident with a transporter in the area, who had asked me to sell him one of my trucks. Upon my refusal, he sent two of his goons to accost me. They pulled out a large knife and would have slit my throat if I had not turned away just in time. It did leave a very deep laceration on my neck, though," he says, lifting his chin to show me the scar underneath it. I gasp slightly.

"I managed to run away from the goons and came across a Weighbridge, where I locked myself into one of the rooms. Thankfully, they could not find me. When I reached home, I called my men and ordered them to find the two goons. I then had both the transporter and the goons arrested and they spent one night in jail, where they were thrashed soundly. The transporter became so frightened that he also left the city."

"These two incidents earned me the reputation of a ganglord much before I became a big transporter. Later on, of course, there were far bigger incidents. I was usually not the instigator, but I would always triumph over my foes. At one time," he says with a smile, "I had almost fifty cases registered against me."

We decide to end the session here and I prepare to leave. But something happened that day which I never spoke about and can only write about now. After Uncle described how Aunty used to meet with the sellers in the verandah where we were sitting, I suddenly felt a presence on the sofa next to me. Although I am not much of a believer in the supernatural, I am convinced that it was Aunty's spiritual being who came and sat with us that day, listening with a smile to her husband's stories about her.

It reminded me later of the lines from Henry Scott Holland's poem The Next Room:

Death is nothing at all.
I have only slipped away to the next room.
I am I and you are you.
Whatever we were to each other,
That, we still are.

Call me by my old familiar name.
Speak to me in the easy way
which you always used.
Put no difference into your tone.
Wear no forced air of solemnity or sorrow.

Laugh as we always laughed
at the little jokes we enjoyed together.
Play, smile, think of me. Pray for me.
Let my name be ever the household word
that it always was.

SANGHARSH

Months have passed and the book is slowly starting to take form, although my ordeals shortly will prevent it from being completed for a long time.

Uncle continues the story of how he came to be venerated and feared.

"As I said, later on, many incidents happened and with each of them, people started believing more and more that I was a big gangster. One of them is quite amusing. Guptaji's house was close to the Taxi Stand. One day, a politician who was close to Guptaji came to the Taxi Stand after meeting him at his house. This politician was also a dreaded criminal and it was said about him that he would chop people's heads off and make them disappear. For no reason at all, he started behaving in a high-handed manner with my men, even brandishing his gun. They did not know who he was and beat him up. I was called there and when I reached, I seized his gun and beat him up some more. Then I threw him under the back seat of a taxi and with my feet upon him (I am pretty sure my expression must have been quite aghast at this moment), we drove to the police station. The Station Officer at that police station was loyal to me: I had got him posted there. By then, I was influential enough to get officials posted here and there. Unfortunately, that day, he was not there and his subordinate took one look at the bruised and bleeding man we had hauled into the police station and almost collapsed. He had recognized the man. Stammering with fright, he asked him what had happened."

"I was puzzled by his obvious fear and deference towards our captive and realized that he was someone important. Then I saw the flashing lights of several police cars which had driven up to the police station and senior police officials emerging from the cars. Seeing that the situation was serious, I immediately called up Guptaji, but before I could narrate the entire incident to him, the phone was snatched away from me, and our captive was handed the phone. He told Guptaji that the taxi drivers had beaten him up severely. Guptaji asked him to let him speak to the policeman in charge at the station, who was instructed that no case was to be registered in the matter and that both parties were to be sent to the Vidhan Sabha (the Legislative Assembly) to meet him."

"Then Guptaji sent his official vehicle to the police station along with the vehicle of a senior Cabinet Minister to take us to the Vidhan Sabha. It was quite a sight," he laughs, "we were in the cars of the Chief Minister and his Cabinet Minister with forty or fifty taxis following us, and all of us were allowed into the Vidhan Sabha without official authorization."

I burst out laughing at the comical image Uncle has conjured up of this motley procession of cars zooming straight into the state Legislature; it seems like a scene out of a Hindi blockbuster movie.

"Once there, we waited along with the Senior Superintendent of Police for Guptaji to arrive, scowling menacingly at each other all the while."

"When Guptaji arrived there after a meeting with the Governor, he heard both parties and then, gesticulating towards me, told my adversary, 'Thakur Sahib (Thakurs being the erstwhile rajas, maharajas, zamindars, and taluqdars of the state), these people are children; what they did was not intentional. Let the matter go.' Then he gently told me to apologise to the politician."

"But the fault was his, I argued, in no mood to be placated, and refused to do what Guptaji had asked, telling him he could send me to jail if he wanted."

"The SSP was shocked at my insolence and catching hold of my shoulder, said menacingly to me, 'Sahib is telling you to...,' but I turned around before he could complete his sentence and said that Guptaji was his Sahib (boss), not mine."

Needless to say, at this point I am mesmerized and intrigued by the story, which still seems to me straight out of a film with an angry young man like Amitabh Bachchan in the lead.

"Guptaji looked at my furious face and turned once again to the politician. With folded hands, he said soothingly to him, 'Let us give in to the children's whims; I apologise to you on their behalf.' That was the end of the matter. Everyone dispersed, but I stayed back, feeling I had hurt Guptaji's feelings. Guptaji went into his private chamber in the Vidhan Sabha, which used to be very spartan in those days. He removed his kurta and dhoti because it was quite warm and lay down on his meager cot to rest. I followed him into the room and apologized for displeasing him. Gutptaji waved me away as I was but an errant child, saying I should go and attend to my business."

I smile at the courage and conviction of my protagonist; two qualities which are so rare these days, and at the special bond that he had shared with the Chief Minister.

"When I returned home from the Vidhan Sabha, I told my wife what had happened. She nonchalantly asked what was new about that, since was I getting into scraps so often. Anyway, the news that I had thrashed the politician-criminal spread like wildfire everywhere, as did the fact that Guptaji had interceded so strongly on my behalf."

"But then C. B. Gupta lost his Chief Ministership once again because of Kamlapati Tripathi's defection from the party and I started facing the brunt of his rivals' simmering resentment and rage."

"First, some roadways people were sent to the Taxi Stand to poach passengers. There was a scuffle at the Taxi Stand and the Circle Officer and Superintendent of Police made a false case against me and others in this matter. Later, of course, the charge sheet against me was quashed because I still had many influential friends and the support of fifteen or sixteen MLAs of the state."

"Then, Malkhani, a man who had been recently appointed the General Manager of Roadways and was very powerful because he was also related to the new Chief Minister, became my foe. He passed an injunction to vacate the Taxi Stand, saying it had been a temporary allotment of land."

"We obtained a stay order for the taxi stand from the court, but the new Chief Municipal Officer, Mahmud Bhatt, who had just got posted to Lucknow was unaware of this stay order and brought a truck full of labourers to the Taxi Stand to begin the demolition. Mahmud Bhatt was quite a force to reckon with; he had carried out many evictions and demolitions with impunity and one of them had even resulted in a fatality. But that day, he bit off more than he could chew. Sixty or seventy of my taxi drivers snatched away the tools and weapons of the labourers and started beating them up. They all tried to run away, including Mahmud Bhatt, but I chased after him and caught him by his collar, which came off in my hand. I then punched him hard."

"When I returned home, my wife looked at my slightly torn clothes and asked who I had fought with that day. I showed her the collar that had torn off and narrated the incident to her. She nodded her head, seemingly unimpressed with my latest scandal."

"After this incident, Mahmud Bhatt called up the SSP in Lucknow to ask him to have us locked up. But the SSP was known to me and told him to file an FIR, which he knew could not be done, as we had already procured a Stay Order for the Taxi Stand. And to make matters worse for him, I filed a Contempt of Court order against him. I remember he was kept waiting under a Neem tree outside the courthouse for a couple of hours before the hearing and that he had to apologise for his actions."

"The next morning, a neighbor ran excitedly into my house with a newspaper, saying that I had been featured in the headlines! I looked at the heading in the newspaper and it said, 'Mahmud Bhatt faces his Waterloo at Charbagh Taxi Stand.'

"Malkhani lost his shirt over this, and I don't mean any pun. He assembled a group of thugs to teach me a lesson. They registered several false cases against me. Then, desperate for revenge, he sent them to my house to have me killed. Luckily, my cow had fallen into a well some distance from the house and I had gone to rescue her, so I had a narrow escape that day. Frustrated at not being able to find me, the thugs shot one of their men and then filed an FIR against me, saying I was the perpetrator of the crime."

"The neighbourhood was soon cordoned off by policemen from the Provincial Armed Constabulary, but I had been forewarned by a policeman I knew well and escaped from there. Some policemen came to my doorstep and demanded that I give myself up. My wife stood coolly at the door and told the policemen to mind their manners because they were talking to a lady. She asked for a search warrant, to which the Senior Inspector said arrogantly that he did not require one."

"Just then, a friend who was a Judicial Magistrate landed up. When he learned of the situation, he told the policemen that B. C. Mishra was not the kind of man to be hiding inside from the police. He requested my wife to allow one of them to search the house and ascertain this for themselves. My wife agreed and the Inspector entered the house. One of my brothers-in-law, who had a congenital heart defect and succumbed to it at quite an early age, was lying down in one of the rooms and he mocked the Inspector, saying he should go and do some real work instead of wasting his time trying to catch me."

"Nonetheless, I could not go back home until my innocence was proved, so another friend of mine who was also a judge gave me sanctuary in his house. On his advice, I wrote an application of surrender which he kept with him, saying that if the police came there looking for me, he would produce the document to prove that I was not a fugitive and had not surrendered only because I feared police brutality."

"When the media got wind of this, they had a field day with it, especially because I was still absconding. Another newspaper published a headline about me, stating that the mafia had become so powerful that they were getting protection from lawmakers!"

"The judge's friend then sent me to stay at the house of a senior lawyer, assuring me that he would arrange bail for me even in the middle of the night if the police came there looking for me. The Chief Judicial Magistrate was not granting me anticipatory bail nor was he taking out an order for my arrest or even seizure of my assets. I could not go back home, even though my third child was on the way. My wife came to meet me secretly a few times, but after the time she was followed and just about managed to evade her pursuers, I told her to stop."

"Meanwhile, protestations had started growing from many influential people about my innocence, especially since it had come to light that the policeman who had filed the false case against me had been bribed with a sum of five thousand rupees. A lawyer for the Malkhani gang, who was the son of the Superintendent of Police from Sultanpur, had been the one to bribe the policeman. The witness in the case was also someone who had been implicated earlier under IPC (Indian Penal Code) Section 307, or Attempt To Murder, although later he would go on to become a Cabinet Minister. At that time, he was studying in Nainital. Strangely, so many different factions came together to destroy what they perceived as my supremacy. Anyway, things reached such an impasse that four or five judges, along with the District Government Council (Criminal), met one night at the house of the lawyer where I had been staying, to decide how to resolve the situation. The DGC Criminal decided that I should write an application to the Chief Judicial Magistrate saying that despite my repeated appeals to either be arrested or be granted bail, nothing had been done. I was a widely recognized face by then, because of who I was and also because of the headlines in the newspapers. He told me I should also attach a photograph of mine from one of the newspapers to prove that a person who was so widely recognizable could not have been able to evade the police for so long."

"I finally managed to get the bail, but the situation remained dire for me. Then, in a big gathering where Chief Minister Kamlapati Tripathi was present along with many MLAs, a very senior and respectable MLA from Basti stood up to say that I was being unduly harassed even though I was innocent. The father of the witness who had helped to falsely implicate me was also an MLA and he was present in the gathering. The judge who had granted bail to his son and also to his son's friend ordered this MLA to recall his son from Nainital. The MLA immediately wrote to his son, instructing him to return at once and I sent a taxi for the son's friend to go to Nainital to fetch him."

"When the son returned, he was compelled by everyone to file an affidavit saying that I was innocent and that he had been coerced to become a false witness in the Attempt to Murder case filed against me. The charges against me were dropped. Now that the charges had been dropped, the Superintendent of Police from Sultanpur was told to bring about a resolution between the two warring factions. A meeting was arranged between me and two prominent people from the enemy camp, with the Superintendent of Police, the Judge, and others present. The two people from the enemy camp were Bakshi and Bhandari, who went on to become the most dreaded criminals in the state. Their enmity with me was basically over control of the Taxi association, but it also rankled them that I had been sheltering men who were their foes. Then, after they had shot their own man to frame me, I had also had the nerve to go over to his house in Alambagh in broad daylight, douse his car with petrol, and set it on fire, shouting all the while for him to come out and face me if he dared. However, they said at the meeting that they were ready for a truce and would even start respecting me as an elder brother, ready to do my bidding whenever their help was required if I stopped protecting those who were opposed to them. I agreed and that was the end of the enmity. I must say that these two always honoured their word. There are not too many such compromises between rival gangs that stand the test of time, but ours did. I did ask for their assistance a few times, such as the time when Doctor Chandravati, who was a friend, asked for my help in evicting squatters from her property. It was not a small matter. There were about three hundred squatters on the property. I told Bakshi and Bhandari that this matter needed to be sorted out and they soon had the squatters thrown off the property. Doctor Chandravati's hospital stands there now."

"When the compromise happened, some criminals who had supported me till then turned against me. They had been harbouring a long-standing grudge against me since the filing of a charge sheet against us involving the roughing up of some Roadways drivers, from which my name had been removed by the authorities because I was influential. One of them appeared at my house one day when I was not there and demanded five hundred rupees from my wife, saying that I would be grievously harmed if she did not pay up, but once again, she refused to be intimidated. She told him he could do whatever he wanted but he would not get a rupee out of her. He left the house but gathered some other criminals and accosted me in front of DAV College. I laughed in their faces and said that their threats did not impress me in the least. Then I shouted that they should try and do their worst. They got scared and ran away."

"What happened to the politician-gangster you thrashed at the Taxi Stand? Did you ever meet him again?" I ask.

"Oh yes," he laughs, "We did meet once at my friend's daughter's wedding. This friend was the Head of Department (Medicine) of the Medical College in Lucknow and treated me like a brother. Murga Maama, as the gangster was called, was my friend's brother-in-law and was shocked to see me at the wedding. He scowled at me furiously, but after learning how close his brother-in-law was to me, he had no choice but to treat me cordially. In later years, his son was very respectful to me and would touch my feet whenever we met."

"As word of my alliance with Bakshi and Bhandari spread, the incidents became fewer and all those who were seeking revenge realized that it was of no use. But I had to fight numerous other battles while I was President of the Taxi Association and later, when I was a Transporter."

"On December 31, 1970, my third daughter Mrinalini was born. This caused a great gloom to descend on the family. Since I did not differentiate between sons and daughters, I told my relatives that there was no reason to mourn, but people started telling my wife how unlucky she was to have borne three girls and some even started avoiding her presence, saying that it was inauspicious for begetting sons. My wife, who had already grieved so much over the son who had died, became very melancholic and would cry a lot. Fearing that she would not properly look after the infant girl she had hoped would be a boy, I started taking care of the baby and making her sleep next to me at night."

"Ironically, it was this very baby girl who changed the course of our destiny for the rest of our lives."

"At the time, I had resigned as the President of the Taxi Association, knowing that it had gained me wrong connections and ill-repute, and resolved to distance myself from any kind of criminal activity. After I withdrew from participation in any kind of unlawful activity, I ceased to have any enmity with anyone, and all the court cases against me slowly got resolved. But it came at a price. I had only one truck operating at that time, the new one that I had bought after selling off the decrepit one, but it was barely enough to make ends meet. Plus, after I had managed to finally pay off the loan on this truck, I foolishly got it re-financed for a friend who needed five thousand rupees, believing that he would pay the loan off. He did not and I was back to square one," he chuckles.

"But only a month after my third daughter was born, a financier from Kanpur who had heard of me asked me if I would help him in recovering loans from defaulters. I agreed and was successful in repossessing the collateral, mostly vehicles, from some very difficult defaulters."

"One night, the financier came over to my place and handed me a briefcase containing twenty thousand rupees, an amount sufficient to purchase a brand new truck. I asked him why he was giving me such a large sum of money and he replied that since I was not taking a salary from him, I could perhaps buy a second truck with the money. 'You can return it to me in installments of five hundred rupees over the next forty months,' he said. He also sent over a Vespa scooter for me, since I no longer had vehicles from the Taxi stand at my disposal, as well as furniture for an office and a telephone."

"Suddenly, I started becoming rich again. I bought another truck and with the income from it, I took out a loan for two more trucks. All this happened within two months of the birth of my third daughter."

"Now that I had a good income coming in, we started upgrading our lifestyle. We renovated the upper portion of the house where my wife and I had once spent a night under a tarpaulin because the unfinished roof leaked in the rain. We finally built a bathroom upstairs and added two more bedrooms. We had mosaic flooring put in and bought expensive draperies."

"We were comfortable and safe, but my wife still longed for a son. Likewise, there was a friend of ours, another Judge, who also longed for a grandson. He was more like a father figure. We used to get together often and play chess."

"You play chess, Uncle," I ask. "Where and when did you learn how to play?"

"Oh, I started playing in our village when I was nine years old and no one has ever beaten me at a game," he replies, "Not even my son-in-law, who I have won three consecutive games from. I learned from the elders in the village. I like the game because one is forced to anticipate the moves of one's opponent in it."

"Anyway, one day we were at the Judge's house when a pundit (Hindu priest) came over to tell him how to go about begetting a grandson. The priest assumed that we were the Judge's son and daughter-in-law. He took my wife's hand to read it and then exclaimed to the judge that his daughter-in-law had an excellent hand and that she would never lack anything in life. 'Your hand predicts untold wealth,' he said, "and I see many cars around you in the future,' he told her. I laughed and asked him if I was going to become a traffic policeman! My wife smiled at me. We had come to the judge's house on our Vespa scooter and our house, although quite luxurious by previous standards, did not even have a garage!"

"But then the priest strangely started describing our house and the Peepal (sacred fig) tree next to it and even told us about a box placed in a certain spot and what it contained. We were amazed. He asked to come over to our house the next day. Once he saw that everything was exactly how he had described it the previous day, he said he would give us a Yagna (a sacred ritual performed with a fire) so that a son would be born to us. He told both the Judge and us to go to a specific place in Fatehpur district and do parikrama (circumambulation) there at a temple of Ambika Devi on the banks of the river Yamuna."

"The Judge and I, along with our spouses, left for Fatehpur the next day in a hired Ambassador car. We had to walk quite a distance to the temple because the car got stuck in the swampy mud next to a canal and it would not budge even though we all tried to pull it out. The temple turned out to be just a rudimentary platform with a few round stones placed on it, but we did the parikrama as we had been told."

"Within a year, we had a son, and the Judge had a grandson. Just before our son was born, the Sikh financier from Kanpur sent over a Fiat car for me. He told me that it was mine to keep; it had been seized from a lawyer who had defaulted on his loan and he said that the lawyer clearly would not be able to fight me in court because of my close friendship with so many Judges. I got it transferred to my name. We had gone to Fatehpur to pray for a son in a hired car that got stuck in the mud and as soon as our son was born, we became the owners of a Fiat car in which we brought him home from the hospital!"

"We started the construction of a proper temple dedicated to Ambika Devi on the spot we had visited because we had vowed to do so if our prayers were answered." "So there is a temple there now?" I ask. "Yes," he answers, "a big temple, visited by many pilgrims. A metalled road now leads to it."

"Does it have your family name on it?" I ask since philanthropy is almost always glorified. "No," he answers, "we never liked that sort of thing. We constructed another temple here in Aliganj after the birth of our son, but it only has a simple plaque with my wife's name on it, stating the reason it was built."

"Guptaji fought his second election from the constituency of Raja Vijay Kumar Tripathi, the Raja of Sesendi, who at the time was still one of the most powerful people in Lucknow. I was very close to the Raja by then and had remained a loyal supporter of C.B. Gupta, so he gave me the charge of managing the entire transport for the second election. Guptaji won the election and on the day that he won, we had a victory procession in front of Charan Singh's house and jeered at him," he smiles. "Then we landed up at Guptaji's house, where he had organized a high tea for us. He thanked all of us personally for his win."

"The Chief Minister and the Transport Minister were both close to me. Special permits were issued to me that allowed my trucks to ply all over the country. I was also issued state permits for the four minibuses that I had also added to my fleet."

"By 1974, I had forty or fifty trucks in my fleet and was one of the wealthiest men of Lucknow. There was black marketing in the chassis of trucks. Trucks cost about thirty or thirty-five thousand and a chassis cost twenty-five or thirty thousand. I booked thirty chassis together at a thousand rupees each, under different names of course, but Hukum Chand Gupta, the dealer, thought that I was going to sell them at black market prices and said he would cancel the order. I told him to go ahead but be prepared to face the consequences."

"Well, I was still considered mafia," he says smilingly. "I was not planning to sell the chassis; I just wanted more vehicles. He did not cancel the order and I obtained the chassis. Having thirty chassis all at once propelled my business because they were normally so hard to acquire."

"The chairman of the Uttar Pradesh Transport Association used to be a powerful appointment and he would usually be made an MLA after his tenure, while the president of the All India Motor Congress would be appointed a Member of Parliament. At that time, the Lucknow Truck Owners Association decided to go on strike. Raj Mangal Pande was the Transport Minister then. Both the Transport Commissioner and Transport Minister's authority was at stake and they knew they would be disgraced if the strike went on for any length of time. They called me to ask me what should be done. I had refused to join the strike. Bakshi was the actual President of the Lucknow Truck Owners Association, but I had told him not to get involved in the strike and so another individual by the name of Gattu had been appointed as President for the duration of the strike."

"Gattu had started getting cargo confiscated from the few trucks that were still operating. I saw this as an opportunity to quash his authority. One night, while he was unloading cargo from a truck, I had him arrested for stealing. The next day, the Chief Judicial Magistrate and the Additional District Magistrate (E) Lucknow were over at my house to inform me that Gattu had been arrested. 'So what,' I said to them, 'Let him relax in jail for a day or two. Cooling his heels in jail will also cool down his very ambitious political game plan.'

"It was a Friday, so they issued an order for Gattu's case to be brought forward on Monday, which meant that he would have to spend three nights in jail. There was a lot of sloganeering in front of my office in Charbagh as Gattu was being taken to the jail from the police station. I asked for him to be brought to me and told him as an aside that he should not apologise to the authorities or back down in any way, even if he had to spend a month in prison!"

We both laugh at this statement and then he continues, "The next day, I was at the CJM's office. I would always be treated with deference whenever I would go there. The lawyer for the Transport Corporation was there and he told me he knew I could easily get Gattu released from prison. I told him I had no personal enmity with Gattu and it was all just politics. Then I told the CJM to not allow Gattu bail for a while. Gattu had to stay in prison for fifteen days," he smiles.

"The President of the Uttar Pradesh Transport Association was very worried after Gattu's arrest. He called me and pleaded with me to save his skin, saying he was ready to do whatever I said. 'Well then, come over to my house,' I told him. He was too scared to even come out of hiding lest he be arrested, so I sent my car over for him. Those days, the Sacchandi Mahayagya was on in my house for the birth of my son. This Yagya goes on for quite a few days and everyone is supposed to circumambulate the Yagya mandap (platform) a hundred and one times. Narayan Baba, as we addressed the President of the UP Transport Association, arrived at my house hidden in the car while the Yagya was going on. The Raja of Sesendi was in my house on that day for the Yagya. I had been a little miffed with him because I had gone over to his house a few days prior and had not been taken in immediately to see him. He had come for the Yagya to placate me. Since he was a Minister in the UP government, there had been quite a few policemen with him and Narayan Baba was horrified to see them and would not get out of the car. I assured him that nothing would happen to him while he was in my house, especially since my relative, the District Judge, was there. 'So even if you are arrested,' I teased him, 'don't worry, you'll get bail immediately.' Then I told him that he had to go around the mandap for the stipulated 101 times while my wife and I went to the temple in Aliganj as we always did every Tuesday. 'Do not stop,' I warned him, 'otherwise you might get arrested.'

"When we returned an hour and a half later, poor portly Narayan Baba had not yet finished the circumambulations and was perspiring profusely. I almost felt sorry for putting him through that ordeal."

"I called the Transport Minister the next day and told him that the strike would be called off, but some individuals had to be released from prison and some others to be given an unconditional pardon before that. He readily agreed. The next day, I took Narayan Baba to his house hidden once again in the back seat of my car, where he begged for pardon and promised the Minister that the strike would end the next day."

"The day after that, Narayan Baba held a large meeting in Charbagh for his supporters where he announced that the Transport Minister had requested a meeting with him, but that he was not going to back down and would state their demands clearly to the Transport Minister when they met. After this brief show of strength, he finally announced the end of the strike. Gattu was released at my request and immediately came to meet me, promising me that he would only do my behest in the future."

"So why did you not join the strike with the others?" I ask him. He replies that he never really liked the Transporters fraternity because they were into black marketing and other fraudulent dealings. "Fleet owners would open their tyre dealerships and petrol pumps because of the fleet owners' quotas. My problem with Narayan Baba started because they had established an illegal monopoly over the market, selling tyres costing a thousand rupees for five thousand rupees. When I objected, he told me that I did not need to worry about either the cost or availability of tyres, but I said I was not thinking of myself; it was just unethical. I had to buy a tyre dealership with a partner because of the huge black marketeering of tyres. However, I stayed away from petrol pumps, because there was just too much unscrupulousness in that business."

"Anyway, when I bought my first minibus, I took about fifty family members and friends for a visit to Allahabad in it," he smiles. "The Superintendent of Police of Allahabad was a very close friend; I now had friends everywhere within the judiciary, police force, and the political arena. At the time, there were fifty-two districts in the state and not one district in which I did not know high-ranking officials and whenever I would travel, arrangements for my stay would be made beforehand by them."

His son has earlier shared with me that in those days, his father would spend most of his time in the Sachivalaya or the Secretariat and the Courts in Lucknow, meeting friends.

"The SP had booked a hotel in Allahabad for us. However, the Chief Justice of the High Court in Allahabad was also a friend and when he learned that we had arrived in Allahabad, he immediately arrived with a bunch of people to receive us. Brusquely, he told the Superintendent of Police who was also in attendance that we would not be staying in a hotel, but in his house. He then took all of us home and ordered food for us from a hotel, apologizing for not serving us a home-cooked meal."

"The mini buses were very profitable, even though the All UP Permit did not allow for individual passengers, only groups of people. But I didn't care. Once the passengers were inside, it was a party," he laughs. "I had all the law enforcement officials in my pocket. I was earning twenty thousand rupees a day (I almost balked at the amount; it was a King's ransom in the early seventies), and my brother-in-law would have to help me to count the money which would arrive in sacks every evening," he chuckles.

"I heard that someone said about me once that the quickest and surest way to get to meet me was to have the cops at any police station stop one of my buses; I would arrive there in no time at all to sort the matter out."

GUROOR

"There is a very interesting incident about how I recovered a stolen vehicle from Nepal," he says when we meet next, and I respond with a smile.

"I had bought a truck on loan and sold it to someone who promised me bigger installments on it: these were all little ways of making some extra money from time to time. Once, this person drove the truck to Nepal, where he unfortunately encountered a gang who thought of killing him and appropriating the truck. A lot of stolen vehicles would end up in Nepal in those days and would never be recovered. Anyway, I learned that the truck had disappeared along with the driver. I deputed my brother-in-law to find out what had happened. When we got to know that the truck had been in Nepal, I set off for Nepal in my car with my wife and the brother and sister-in-law of the driver. In Nepal, I was able to locate the truck with the help of some local officials, who promised me that they would assist me in recovering the truck and helping it cross the border into India. Once the truck reached Nanpara, the first border town in India, I knew I would be home safe."

"The ladies were shopping in the town of Nepalgunj when the Nepalese officials I had contacted hurried up to us and said the truck had been found. We had to make a quick getaway. We had barely managed to get into our car when the men who had spirited the truck away came running towards us, brandishing swords in their hands. They struck our car repeatedly, but we managed to drive off unscathed. They chased us to the border, where, if the driver of the truck had not crashed through the barrier and entered India with us in tow, we would have been caught by our pursuers. Unfortunately, because we had crashed through the barrier, the Nepalese police radioed police officials in India, saying that a stolen truck from Nepal had just entered India with a cargo of marijuana."

"Fortunately, I knew the Superintendent of Police of Bahraich very well. Bahraich is very close to Nanpara. I explained to the deputation of Indian policemen waiting for us at Nanpara that the truck had not been stolen but recovered. I asked them to verify my credentials with the Superintendent of Police. But they insisted that we had to go to the police station with them till my antecedents were verified. I was angry about being taken to the police station after I had told the policemen of my relationship with the SP, and because there were two ladies with us, but I had to comply. To our amazement, however, at the police station, they sat us down for tea and refreshments and joked that they could not possibly have let a friend of the SP go away without availing of their hospitality. After tea, they escorted us to the river Ghagra and radioed the Nepal police to tell them that the truck was not carrying any contraband and had not been stolen from Nepal."

"Just one question, Uncle," I can't help saying, "What were Aunty and the other lady doing with you on such a dangerous mission?"

"Oh, they were just excited about shopping in Nepal," he replies with a shrug, quite oblivious to the incredulity of the situation.

"There is another very interesting story from around that time. I had recovered a truck from a defaulter on behalf of the Sikh financier. The defaulter lodged a case against the financer's company, Sardar Finance Corporation, and nine others including my wife and me, under Sections 395, 468, 465, 471, 12-B/34 of the Indian Penal Code. (I marvel when he recites these perfectly from memory). The case was filed because the amount advanced by the financier, about half of the total purchase cost of the truck, was by way of a loan which had enabled the appellant to acquire the truck, while according to the financier, it was based on a Hire purchase agreement which had been executed in writing. The complainant also declared that the agreement entered on 29th March 1973 was not duly filled up and that his signature had also been obtained on a blank form. It was further stated by him that the accused had acted in a high-handed manner and during his absence had come to his house, where despite protests from his wife, had forcibly removed the truck under threat of arms and committed dacoity. This, he said, was even though two monthly installments out of the total of twenty-three had already been paid by him and the third installment was due on July 31, 1973, but the accused acted against him before the due date."

"The Magistrate passed an issue of Summons against all of us accused. On the same day, after the Summons was issued, we moved the Allahabad High Court to quash the Criminal proceedings, but the High Court dismissed our application. Against this order, we filed an appeal before the Supreme Court."

"The Supreme Court reversed the judgment and held that the case was one where none of the processes ought to have been directed to be issued against the accused and purely on the well-settled principles of law, it was a suitable case where the criminal proceedings ought to have been quashed by the High Court in the exercise of its inherent power. It also stated that the dispute raised by the appellant was purely civil, even assuming the facts stated by him were substantially correct! Furthermore, assuming that the agreement had not been duly filled up and that his signature had been obtained on a blank form, this was in no way an offense of forgery or the like and could only be an offense if the paper had been fabricated into a document of the kind which attracts the relevant provisions of the Penal Code or when such a document was used as a genuine document. Under the Hire Purchase agreement, the Financer had made the payment of a huge sum of money and he was the owner of the vehicle, and on default of any monthly installment, he had the right to terminate the Hire Purchase agreement even without notice and seize the truck."

"In conclusion, the Supreme Court stated that the case was a bona fide civil dispute which led to the seizure of the truck and that the highly exaggerated account of the complainant that the appellants went to his house with a mob armed with deadly weapons and committed the offense of dacoity in taking away the truck was very unnatural and untrustworthy because nobody on the side of the respondent was hurt."

"This judgment ended up being one of the landmark judgments on Hire Purchase Agreements: Trilok Singh Vs Satya Dev Tripathi 1979 SC 850."

Even before I can respond in total admiration, he continues: "My trucking company, named Mishra Sardar Transport Corporation (because the Sikh gentleman from Kanpur had helped in the setting up of the company) was running twenty trucks to Calcutta every day, and the rest mainly to Jhansi, with freights of coal from Ranchi. Big transporters were courted by politicians and treated with great respect by them because they could provide vehicles for their rallies and campaigns. However, the Mishra Sardar alliance did not last. My partner had been buying tyres with black money and selling them at inflated prices. When the black marketeering in tyres stopped, his profits started drying up and he said he wanted to exit the transport business. We had suffered a lot of losses in the business by then and I would not have been able to repay my debts even by selling all the vehicles, but I still took on all the assets and liabilities of the company. Only fifteen days later, the price of trucks increased by fifteen or twenty thousand rupees and since I now had forty trucks, I prospered from the deal after all."

"Meanwhile, the Judge who had helped me secure bail had now become the Registrar of the High Court in Allahabad and since he was responsible for the transfers of civil judges, he had great power and authority. He came to my assistance twice after being appointed Registrar of the High Court. The first time was when a Magistrate, whom I had helped to rent the house of my friend, stopped paying rent and instead threatened the landlord with legal action!"

"I called up my friend the Registrar to tell him about the Magistrate's behaviour, and he immediately issued a transfer order for him. I then went over to the Magistrate's house and shouted out from the street that he should pack his bags and get ready to move and that whatever warrant he was going to issue against the landlord or even me, he could do from his new place of posting!"

"The second time the Registrar helped me was when the new Judicial Magistrate in Lucknow told me to travel to Sitapur to settle my cases of transport fines, which previously were being handled in Lucknow itself. When I told him that I never had to travel to Sitapur before about the fines, he called me into his chambers and told me that he did not care to do my bidding and goaded me to get him transferred out of Lucknow if I thought I was powerful enough to do so."

"He did not think that I would manage it, but at my request, my friend in Allahabad issued a transfer order for him as well. The Judicial Magistrate was furious and travelled to Allahabad to protest against the transfer, telling the Registrar that he knew it had been done on my behest, but the Registrar said that his posting had been overdue after three years in Lucknow and asked him how he had dared to come to Allahabad to meet him without taking permission from the District Judge first. 'I can suspend you for this,' he told the JM. 'Leave quietly now and I might be willing to transfer you to a place of your choice, but you are not continuing in Lucknow.'

"This Magistrate used to be so arrogant that when the Deputy Law Minister visited the courts, he did not even stand to greet him and when questioned about it, answered that he was not in the employ of the Minister and could even file a Contempt of Court order against him for asking him to do so."

"So," he says with a laugh, "it was more for his arrogance than my ego that I got him transferred out of Lucknow, otherwise I would not have bothered. I would generally hesitate to approach anyone for favours. Once, an accident claim involving one of my trucks landed on the docket of a Judge named Shahi. He was a close friend. Not knowing that it was my vehicle that was involved, he ruled that the claim in lieu of the accident was valid. I appealed the matter in the High Court, but it was later resolved through a compromise. When he came to know this entire saga, he was very upset. He came to my house and asked why I could not have simply told him at the start that the claim involved my truck. 'I would have sorted it out right away,' he said. I smiled and told him that I did not want preferential treatment. He shook his head in disbelief."

"But that was the way it was. It may have created delays and hurdles in many instances, but my self-respect meant everything. Prabhat Kumar, the Home Secretary who went on to become the Cabinet Secretary of India once told me at my farm that it was one of the most peaceful and relaxing places to be because one never encountered any photographers or sycophants there. 'Indeed,' I said, 'I have never called any of you here because you are powerful or because I can glean favours from you. Come here if you want to relax and have a good time, otherwise don't.' I heard later that quite a few people were appalled at my brusqueness."

"The fact that I had got two judges posted out in a month, one of them being the pompous Magistrate, further enhanced my image in the eyes of people. Not only were the biggest gangsters of the time like my younger brothers who would do anything for me, but I was very closely connected with powerful members of the Judiciary as well."

"At that time, did you already own both the houses in Rajindernagar?" I question him, trying to form a timeline of events in my mind.

"No, at that time, we had only one house and there was an empty plot next to it. I used to tie my cow in the empty plot." (I can't help smiling at my subject's love for cattle). "I asked the owner many times to sell it to me, but he let it be known that he would sell it to anyone but me. I could not understand this unreasonable stance. Finally, I told him that no buyer would ever dare to buy the plot from him, because no one had the guts to go and untie my cow from there. The owner still did not budge and even sent over a group of men to the plot to start construction. Seeing this, I called fifty of my men to send them packing. They rushed to the police station to complain, but no one at the station would listen to them and they were told to go on their way."

"But since I did want to buy the plot, I asked my men to look for the owner's Achilles heel. They discovered that there was a pending vigilance case against him. I had the case re-opened and had a message sent to him that he could either sell me the plot or face time in prison for that case."

"He was finally left without a choice and he came to me, saying that he would sell the plot to me for a little more than the two lakhs I had initially offered to him. Since he had unnecessarily denied me so many times, I refused to pay the amount and told him I would give him a pittance instead. However, my wife had been listening and taking pity on him, she asked me to at least give him the amount he had paid for the plot plus a fixed deposit interest on the amount, so I did end up paying him forty-seven thousand rupees even though I could have bought the plot for almost nothing."

"Within two months, we had built a huge house on the plot with a massive drawing room, bedroom, and bathroom. My brother, who was a Chief Engineer by then and a friend who was the Registrar of the High Court would visit us often and our first house could not properly accommodate them, even with its seven or eight bedrooms; so I was happy we now had adequate space for all our guests."

"Did you ever think that your life story reads like the script of a film, Uncle?" I ask laughingly.

"I never thought of it, no," he replies seriously. "All I ever wanted was respect in society, especially within my Brahmin community and I am proud to say that I achieved this in my life."

PARAKRAM

"It still surprises me that I became so entrenched in and a part of the VVIP culture of Lucknow: something that was unimaginable when I started as a young man. But then, I had become one of the city's wealthiest men and was close to the biggest politicians, judges, and bureaucrats as well as the most infamous criminals like Bakshi and Bhandari and later Hari Shanker Tiwari, Pandit Ram Gopal, Anna, and others," Uncle continues from where we had left off last time.

"When my wife wanted to get our son admitted into the prestigious St. Francis College," he reflects, "we approached the Superintendent of Police (City) to talk to the Principal on our behalf. It took him seventeen or eighteen meetings with the Principal to finally get our son admitted. However, only a few years later, my influence ensured that I could walk into the school at any time and meet the Principal, no matter how busy he was."

"How did you get so close to him, Uncle?" I wonder, and he replies with a shrug that the Principal and pretty much everyone else knew that Bakshi and Bhandari called him elder brother and that certain other well-known gangsters were so deferential to him that they would touch his feet when they met him."

"But," he says, "I also helped out the Principal in a case related to the school in which he was implicated," he adds mysteriously, without divulging any details.

"To think that I once had tea with a constable and came back home elated and told my wife that I had powerful connections!" he laughs.

"Were there any more encounters such as the ones you have described before?" I want to know, referring to unsavoury incidents with goons and the like.

"There are too many to recall," he replies. Then, after thinking for a bit, he says, "At one point, the Chief Medical Superintendent of Northern Railways was staying on the upper floor of our Rajendernagar house. He had become like a family member to us and only vacated our house reluctantly when the Railways ordered him to move into the official residence on its campus. He had arranged the marriage of his nephew to the niece of the Director General of Police but then called it off for some reason. The DIG took this as a personal insult and along with his friend who was the Deputy Commissioner of Sales Tax, sent goons over to our house to rough up the CMS and his nephew. When they arrived at the house, the duo was sitting with us as they usually did in their free time. The goons started manhandling all of us and even tried dragging the nephew away with them. My wife and daughter sustained injuries before I had a chance to summon my men. I always had forty or fifty men on standby. I was also injured and bleeding. When a truckful of my men landed up from Charbagh, we finally chased the goons away. The news of this incident travelled fast and the SP City and DM City landed up at my house and told me to file an FIR against the goons. I instructed them to go and apprehend the criminals first. They left immediately and found out that the DIG, the Deputy Commissioner, and their lawyer were at the venue of a function in Mahanagar. They reached the venue, surrounded it, and arrested all three. It was then that I lodged an FIR against them."

"A Judge of the High Court was both a relative of theirs and my friend. He stepped in to mediate, knowing that both parties were powerful and things could get ugly. He agreed that there had been a grave error on the part of the DIG and his friend and asked me how the situation could be resolved."

"Severe punishment," I answered. 'What kind of punishment?' he asked me. I told him to decide the punishment, keeping in mind that they had not only come into my house and attacked us without provocation; the ladies of my household had been injured in the attack." 'As for me,' I said, 'even if they only come to my house and ask for forgiveness from Doctor Gupta and the ladies of my family, the feud will be over from my side.'

"The Judge took me to the police station with him, where the miscreants were being held. Upon seeing us together, it was obvious to all that he was not going to blindly side with his relatives. Their supporters got worried and begged him for a fair decision. 'Mr. Mishra is a better judge of the situation,' he answered them tersely, 'and he will decide what is to be done.' Then he drove off in his car. They were shocked and started pleading with me to forgive the perpetrators. I told them exactly what I had told the Judge and then had them released. No one could believe that I was letting them off the hook so easily. The perpetrators came to my house and begged forgiveness from the Doctor. Then they fell at my wife's feet and apologized profusely for the fact that they had hurt the women. I ended the matter after that; I knew that if I had let things escalate, the fact that both of us were equally powerful would have led to disastrous consequences."

"Did Papa tell you about his Mafioso days?" his son, walking into the room and hearing the conversation, asks me with a wink.

"Yes, I know of many incidents that catapulted him to gang leader status," I smile and answer. "Do you know about the time Papa beat up the telephone line guy?" he asks laughingly and adds that the guy complained later to the police that B.C. Mishra kept beating him and serving him tea in between beatings.

I laugh at the incredulousness of this and tell him I have never heard any story of a person being beaten and also being served tea.

"In 1980, we had fixed line telephones in our Charbagh office," Uncle reluctantly elaborates. "You probably know that India's telecom network was not vastly developed then and telephones were only available to the corporate sector and a small section of households. It was also notoriously unreliable. Telecommunications were a government monopoly until 1994 when liberalisation gradually started taking place. Well, there was a local union of telephone linesmen to whom I would pay fifty rupees a day just to ensure that the telephones remained operational, as our work depended heavily on them."

"I realized after some time that they would purposely tamper with the lines to make extra money out of us. It made me very angry but we could not afford to say or do anything about it. However, one day, an altercation took place regarding this between my nephew and one of the linesmen. I was not in the office at the time. By the time I came in, the linesman was being beaten up. Five or six of his colleagues tried to come to his aid, but I had about fifteen employees in the office and they were no match for us. The beating lasted for quite a few hours, but we did allow them to take breaks for tea."

I laugh loudly and he says, "Of course, another FIR was lodged against me, in which they mentioned all the details of the incident, including the tea breaks."

He smiles at his own story. "I got the FIR quashed, but they later went and complained to their Senior Divisional Engineer and announced that they would go on a city-wide strike because of what had happened. When I learned that they were threatening a strike, I let them know that not only would I gather them all and beat them up again, but this time I would oust them from the city. Hearing this, they went to an even more senior official for redressal, but he also did nothing and in fact, came over to my Charbagh office to thank me for being the only person who had ever managed to bring that rowdy and undisciplined lot to heel."

"I was a bit too free with my fists those days if I felt someone was trying to cheat me or fool me," he says a bit self-consciously. "In the Rajendernagar house, there was a heated argument with the man who would come to read the electricity meter and I gave him a couple of slaps too. He also went to file an FIR against me, but the policemen were so used to this kind of thing being an everyday matter with me that they waved him away without even listening to the details."

"One night, my wife and I were returning after attending a function at the house of the Superintendent of Police in Unnao. Just as we were entering our colony, we saw that all the roads had been blocked by huge crowds of people, apparently because a murder had taken place there. There were also hordes of policemen present."

"Almost immediately, I suspected foul play and a conspiracy against me. There were still a lot of petty criminals who wanted to get the better of me. On Holi that year, there had been a quarrel between two local gangs and all the individuals had been arrested. I called up the police station and told them to release everyone. One of the gangs was loyal to me and its members had jeered at the members of the other gang, saying that if their benefactor B. C. Mishra had not intervened, they would have been in jail indefinitely."

"That night, we were returning in the private vehicle of the SP, because I had lent my car to the Inspector General of Police, Lal Singh Verma, who needed to visit a relative in hospital every day. The SP had sent an Inspector with us as well, because there were a lot of kidnappings those days, but we had dropped him off at the toll on the outskirts."

"It was almost providential that the car in which we were travelling and my car carrying the IGP had crossed each other on the way to Unnao. Both vehicles had slowed down and we had waved out to each other. This was proof of the fact that we had been on our way to Unnao at the time."

"When one of the police inspectors saw me, he came running towards me and told me to get out of the area immediately. He said that the men who had committed the murder had shouted out loudly in the colony, 'Long live B. C. Mishra,' and everyone now assumed I was behind the murder, especially the brother of the deceased, who had smeared a 'tilak' on his forehead, swearing to exact revenge for the death of his brother. He had filed an FIR against me for murder, but the police officials had been told that the IGP himself had seen me while on my way to Unnao and one of the inspectors informed him that the murder charge would not stand. He then filed a second FIR in which he stated that I had not committed the murder myself, but had arranged it. What he did not know is that one cannot file cross/counter FIRs providing contrasting narratives of the same incident and that doing so can be treated as an offense. The SP, who was my friend, ordered the brother to be arrested and jailed."

"The brother had not expected this turn of events and started begging forgiveness, whereupon the SP told him that he should file a third FIR with an accurate representation of events. He agreed readily. My name was not mentioned in the third FIR, because I had had no connection with the murder."

"The brother was subsequently released. But I did still have the threat of retribution looming over my head and started carrying gunmen with me all the time. After a few weeks, this situation became unacceptable to me and I decided to end the matter. I took ten gunmen to his house in broad daylight and told him that he had filed a false murder case against me, but now his family or friends could file a true FIR against me for murder because I was going to kill him. His Uncle fell at my feet and pleaded with me to forgive his nephew. The brother saw I was serious and also went down on his knees, saying that he had done wrong, but would never do such a thing again."

"After that day, I never had to worry about the brother, although he was intrinsically a bad character and later started using drugs. Every once in a while, he would land up like a beggar at my Charbagh office and I would hand him some money because, after all, he had lost his brother."

How could he forget to tell me this grave story in the course of his narrative, I wonder. If I had not prodded him, would he have even remembered? How many such stories were there?

Oblivious to my amazement, he says, "Ten days after my compromise with Bakshi and Bhandari, the duo shot a man in broad daylight and managed to get away with it. Their notoriety kept growing with their crimes, but they eventually faced a tragic end. Unlike them, however, I chose to extricate myself from a life of crime and become a respectable householder, which is why I am here before you today. Who knows how it may have ended otherwise?"

"I never harmed anyone or wanted to. I have even employed people who were against me for years, though I have often been warned against this. But my thinking is different. Enmity is easy, forgiveness isn't. And forgiveness always leads to reconciliation and peace."

I must admit I agree with the bit about not employing your enemies and having them so close to you, even though I am a huge proponent of forgiveness.

"Many years ago, without even telling me, my wife gave two lakh rupees to an electrician who worked for us so that he could buy a plot of land for himself to secure his future. She got it registered under the name of one of our Managers, who is from the Scheduled caste and whom I employed even though he waged court battles with me for four years to extract money from me." Not noticing my wide-eyed expression of disbelief, he goes on, "First, the Manager enlisted the help of two other individuals from his caste to get me to succumb and when that did not work, burned down his own house and filed an FIR against me with the help of a legislator he knew, charging me for the crime. This was in 1990. I drove to the police station the next morning with the Deputy Superintendent of Police and presented myself to be arrested. The policemen were astonished and said that they could not do that without conducting their enquiries first as the Raja of Sesendi and I were the two most eminent people in the area. The next day, I received a call from the Senior Superintendent of Police who requested me to come to his office to discuss the case. I told him I was just back from work, so I would rest a bit and meet him later in the evening. Meanwhile, the Inspector General (Zone) reached my house and told me we would go and sort out the matter together. We left for the SSP's office and he stood up respectfully to receive us when we reached. Taking the SSP with us, we then drove to Mohanlalganj in the IG's car. The SSP was sitting in front of the IG's car, while the IG and I were sitting at the back. The SSP's car followed the IG's car. My car was in the vanguard behind the official vehicles. I had told the IG that it was beneath him to get personally involved in this matter, but he said that it was also beneath the legislator to get involved in this matter. When we arrived at the police station at Mohanlalganj, the SSP hauled up the inspector there for having registered a case against me. The Inspector pleaded that the legislator had forced him to do so and that they had intended to carry out a full inquiry. The SSP told him that the case registered against me was patently false and since the law required that a person who filed a wrongful case should be penalized, he should file a new FIR against the Manager. Usually, this would have been done with the permission of the DM and the SP, but the SSP told the inspector that he had his permission and the consent from the DM would arrive shortly."

"The case against me was thrown out. Later, the Inspector got in touch with me and begged me to arrange a meeting for him with the

IG. I told him he could come to my farmhouse in plainclothes that very evening, where the IG had been invited. He was delighted at the opportunity to get up close and personal with the IG, especially because the IG told him that if he ever wanted anything from him, he could let me know."

"Despite all that had happened, I still ended up hiring that individual from the Scheduled Caste as the Manager for my farm. Many people told me I was making a mistake and that he was not to be trusted, but I wanted to give him a chance at redemption. I would even joke with him when I visited the farm that he should stand directly in front of me and never behind me because that way he could not stab me in the back!"

"Unfortunately, the Manager was apparently beyond redemption. As of today, he is refusing to transfer the plot of land to the electrician because it is now worth forty lakhs. The poor electrician could never have thought he would be defrauded; after all, the land had been given to him by 'Jagat Didi' (the benefactress of all)."

"So how are you going to solve this problem now?" I interject.

"Oh, I will have to tell him that if he does not do as asked, he might find it very difficult to continue living where he is," he says unperturbedly.

SAMMAN

"I saw stupendous success between 1970 and 1980 and made the turnaround towards a respectable life, but in 1979, I was made acutely aware of the notorious reputation I still carried when my daughter Gudiya (Madhulika) got married to a boy who was employed with the Indian Railway Service. Her marriage had earlier been fixed to a boy from Allahabad, but we decided that this match was better because the boy from Allahabad was working with the Reserve Bank of India, which meant that our daughter would be permanently based in Bombay; while the Railway Service had postings all over the country. Bombay was almost like a foreign land back then. There were no flights and trains would take three days to reach Bombay from Lucknow!"

"Once this match was fixed, my wife and I kept asking the boy's parents to tell us what dowry they would like, but each time, they said they did not want any dowry from us. Finally, the father of the boy said that they had no demands at all and I could give my daughter whatever I wished."

"It was the first wedding in the family and a host of bigwigs attended it. When the bride and groom were departing, police vehicles escorted their car all the way," he says with a smile.

"Just before the marriage, the Director General of Police had told my daughter's in-laws that they were getting their son married to the daughter of a goon. He had wanted to marry his daughter to the boy. Whatever my daughter's in-laws may have thought of that, they still went ahead with the wedding. Ironically, when my second daughter got married in 1983, this time to a boy in the Provincial Civil Service who was later inducted into the Indian Administrative Service, we discovered that the DGP who had tried to sully my reputation was related to the boy! It was indeed a very awkward situation for him, but when he met me at the wedding, he made up a story about how he had earlier mistaken me for a criminal with the same name!"

"My second daughter's marriage was fixed by Gopinath Dixit, a Minister in the State Government who had become a close friend. As in the case of my eldest daughter, we did not have to go looking for a groom. He suggested the boy to us because he was known to him and had a good job in Indian Railways. Even Pinky's (Meenakshi, their second daughter) wedding had been fixed with a boy from Kanpur, who had cleared the Indian Police Service examination and was undergoing training in Hyderabad. The boy and girl had still to meet when I changed my mind. The boy landed unannounced at my office when he got to know I had called off the match and said he wanted to meet my daughter. I calmly told him her marriage had been fixed elsewhere. He became very agitated and demanded that their wedding go through, but I asked him why he was so insistent when there had been no formal ceremony and he had never even met the girl. Besides, who was to say that he would not have changed his mind later? In any case," I then said firmly, "I will get my daughter married to whomever I deem fit." The boy was very upset and his family held great resentment towards us for a long time, but I did not care because I had far more clout than they did and they knew they could not retaliate."

"The marriage of Bobby (Mrinalini) also happened without any effort from our side. The boy's elder brother and my son-in-law were batch mates in the Railways and when they came to know that they had an eligible girl as well as an eligible boy in their families, they decided to get them together. Without telling us, they got their horoscopes matched and when it was found that the boy and girl were compatible, they started celebrating amongst themselves and only informed us of it later!"

"Seeing that it was a good match, my wife and I set off for Hardoi to meet the boy's parents, but upon reaching there, learned that they were in Lucknow, so we returned to Lucknow. Those days, I used to consume a lot of Pan Parag (a well-known brand of mouth freshener those days which was made from betel nuts, cardamoms, lime, and catechu and had a famous television advertisement in which a groom's family's only request from the bride's family was to welcome the groom's side with Pan Parag).

When we met up, the boy's father said there really was nothing for us to discuss as his son and my son-in-law had already deemed the match to be an excellent one, so I told him to take out some Pan Parag for me. We all laughed at the joke and the wedding was finalized."

"Betu's (Malvika's) marriage was arranged with a Doctor through a matrimonial advertisement unlike her sisters, but even in her case, the boy's parents told us on our very first meeting that they liked our daughter and us so much that we could take their son away with us right there and then!"

"After our son was born, the priest who had told us to go to Fatehgarh to pray for a son told us that another son would be born to us, but we had our fourth daughter instead. I have always felt, however, that she has been like a son to me. She has always been independent and ambitious and she paved her way towards becoming a renowned surgeon, even going to Germany by herself for her studies."

"Despite the ease with which all my daughters were married into such respectable families, I had not been able to shake off my notoriety. In 1984, I had met a Jat police officer who made me realize I needed to change my image when he said that fleet owners were considered an 'illiterate moneyed lot' by society. It was insulting, but I could not deny that it was probably true. While a lot of us had enormous wealth, we did not have any kind of social standing. Also, there was too much rivalry between big transporters, which sometimes escalated into outright gang wars. At one time, one of my rivals started plying his buses on my route. Before I could react, my wife had driven out to rectify the situation. She stopped one of the buses on our route. It was full of passengers. She had the driver pulled out and tied to a tree and sent off the passengers in one of our buses. Then she sent out word to the owner of the bus that he could recover his bus and driver from there if he had the guts to do so."

We both laugh heartily and he continues that the feud did carry on for a few days with the rival still trying his best to usurp that route, but eventually, he was told by the police to back off. Left with no choice, he asked that he be given a week to withdraw, lest he lose face. After that, things soon went back to normal."

"Strangely, before this incident," he reflects, "I had had no problem with this particular rival. I even respected him like an elder brother and whenever I would meet his wife, I would joke with her to give me a rupee from her purse as a token to her husband's younger brother. He had quite a similar regard for me. After the dispute was settled by the police, I met his wife at the Regional Transport Office. She said candidly to me, 'Mishra, unlike my husband, whom you respect like an elder brother, you are an educated man. Stop this enmity. From now on, whatever he does, do not react.' I respectfully acquiesced to her request. When I later met him at a common friend's gathering, I greeted him warmly and touched his feet, upon which he placed an arm around my shoulder. That was the end of our rivalry."

"Anyway, coming back to the Jat police officer, he suggested that I start investing in farmland to exit the transport business. He told me that Eucalyptus farming was becoming popular because it was so lucrative and advised me to buy land and plant Eucalyptus trees on it. 'You will soon become a crorepati (multi-millionaire),' he said. I was already very wealthy but a crore in those days was still a very big amount and the idea appealed to me even more because I could become respectable in the process. Back in the days when I was still growing my business, I had visited an astrologer with one of my brothers and he had told me that I would become a lakhpati (millionaire) one day. I had returned home and excitedly told my wife about the prophecy, believing it would come true. But even though that prophecy had come true, it was still hard for me to believe that I could become a crorepati."

"Overnight, I changed the course of my destiny. The very next day after my conversation with the Jat police officer, I woke up in the wee hours of the morning and drove out to the outskirts of the city, scouting for land. I bought ten acres of land at nine thousand rupees an acre that day."

"In October that year, I had gone to my farmland to supervise the boring on it when I heard the news that Prime Minister Indira Gandhi had been assassinated by her own Sikh guard. There were a lot of big Sikh farmers in the area then. Fearing retribution in the aftermath of the assassination, many of them sold their lands at throwaway prices and fled. I paid earnest money for a hundred and fifty acres of land which was being sold for only three or four thousand rupees an acre. I had decided that I would sell off my trucks one by one to pay for the remaining amount. I also advised some of my close friends to buy land. I truly did not believe that I was taking advantage of the distress selling: it was just a business transaction between seller and buyer."

"I thus became the owner of more than a hundred and fifty acres of land. I also had a windfall with the ten acres of land on which I had planted Eucalyptus. In less than two years, the price of the land escalated from nine thousand rupees an acre to a lakh an acre because of the Eucalyptus plantation. I bought the land for a lakh and a half rupees and sold it for twenty-two lakhs! With that money, I was able to pay off the whole amount for the hundred and fifty acres of land I had bought. I did start selling off my trucks, but now it was to buy more land. In 1989, seeing how much landholding I had, the District Magistrate tried to get me to sell twenty acres to him, but I flatly refused to sell even an acre."

"By 1990, I had sold off my entire fleet, and my money was all tied up in landholdings, so I had a huge cash crunch. It was then that a very wealthy businessman friend of mine approached me with an offer. In their family, it was decreed that only sons could inherit the family assets and he only had two daughters. He didn't want to lose his fortune to his brother's sons, so he suggested adopting our only son, telling me it was going to be a mere formality and that my son would inherit his fortune. Despite the precarious financial position I was in, I could not think of such a thing and told him that my wife would not allow it because she had yearned for a son for too many years."

"Despite my refusal, the gentleman handed over fifty thousand rupees to me, saying it was to help me tide over my crisis and I could return it after my Eucalyptus plantations had been harvested. When I did eventually return the money, I wanted to pay him the interest on it as well, but he told me he would not accept interest from his younger brother."

"He remained a very good friend of the family. He had car dealerships and would send over a new car for me nearly every fifteen days so that I never had to buy a car for myself and everyone in the city thought that I was wealthy enough to change my cars every fortnight, or I was into smuggling of cars!"

"When I bought this bungalow," he says, probably remembering events from that period, "I had also bought another bungalow in the cantonment, which I handed over to Mayawati, who went on to become the Chief Minister of the state."

"How did that happen?" I ask him.

"Well, Satish Mishra, who was her aide and a relative of ours, had promised Mayawati that he would help her get a bungalow in the cantonment. However, he had been unsuccessful in his endeavour. He told me sadly that he had not been able to keep his promise to her. My wife heard this and brought the keys of the bungalow to him, telling him that the bungalow was now his. He was astonished and asked her the price of the bungalow. My wife replied that the price was a currency note of the least denomination that he had on him at that moment."

"Satish Mishra was ecstatic and went to Mayawati to tell her that her wish had been fulfilled because of us. She was very happy, but asked that the bungalow remain in my name, as there were too many complications regarding renovations of bungalows in the cantonment and she did not want the hassle."

"Once she moved into the house, I went over to meet her. I found her looking very morose and I guessed that the reason for it was her political prospects at the time. I told her that the house would prove very lucky for her and she would soon become the Chief Minister of the state. At the time, she was nowhere in the reckoning for the Chief Ministership, but my prophecy did come true and she did become Chief Minister. On the fourth day after assuming oath, she called my wife and me over to her official residence for tea and expressed her gratitude. As we were about to leave, she pointed to an official car in the driveway with a red beacon light on top and said that it was mine because she was making me a Minister in her government, but we told her with folded hands that we were content with our lives and did not want any political appointment. She insisted, saying that it was my blessing that had made her Chief

Minister, but I said that it was the Almighty who had decided it; I had only wished well for her from my heart."

"If I did have any political aspirations, I could have fulfilled them much earlier when C. B. Gupta offered to make me an MLA," he explains.

"It is true that I have always wished well for people from the bottom of my heart and without any self-interest. It happened with Ram Kumar as well, who was Mayawati's Appointment Secretary. He was removed from office by the President of India at the behest of Kalyan Singh, who had become the Chief Minister after Mayawati. Ram Kumar was distraught and I consoled him and told him not to worry. He asked me how he could not worry: his career was finished because he had been dismissed by the President. I told him that sometimes things happen in mysterious and unexpected ways. Then I spontaneously said that he would be reinstated and that he should promise to visit a certain place with me when it happened. He was disbelieving but agreed. Six months later, he won a court case for unfair dismissal and was reappointed."

"He came over to the house with his first salary after reinstatement and asked me where I would like to go to celebrate. I reminded him that he had agreed to accompany me to a certain place when his problem had been resolved and we left for the Hanuman temple in Aliganj, which my wife and I would visit every Tuesday. We had so much faith in that temple that many of our friends, like Justice Johri, who was able to get out of his own embroilment, had started worshipping there and experienced similar miracles in their lives."

"When Bobby's husband was posted in Pithoragrah (a town in the Himalayas), my wife and I went there to visit them. Bobby couldn't handle the cold and my wife was worried about her. One day, when Ram Kumar came over to our house, she asked him if there was something he could do to get our son-in-law posted out of Pithoragarh. I interjected, telling her that a young officer like Bobby's husband needed to have a high altitude posting and there was nothing anyone could do about it, but Ram Kumar told my wife to give him a day to see if he could manage it. He then went to Mayawati, who was the Chief Minister, and told her that he needed a favour for someone who was like family to him. He explained about the posting, saying that he was aware that it was mandated for two years as per government policy. Mayawati asked him impassively who the head of the government in the state was. 'The Chief Minister, of course, Madam,' he replied. 'And who is the Chief Minister?' she asked. 'Why, you, of course, Madam,' he replied. 'Exactly,' she said, and told him to get her the file of the officer concerned."

"Our son-in-law was immediately transferred out from Pithoragarh to Rae Bareilley. This caused hostility between him and the District Magistrate there, who was miffed that he had managed the posting using political influence and that he had not even waited for his successor to arrive in Pithoragarh before moving out. He threatened him with suspension. My son-in-law's brother informed me of this and I told Ram Kumar about it. He called up the Chief Secretary of the state and told him that the order for transfer had come directly from the Chief Minister's office and that if anyone even remotely questioned it, they would be summoned for violating a government order."

"The next morning, I received a call from my son-in-law, saying he had been officially relieved of his duty in Pithoragarh and the District Magistrate had personally taken charge of the appointment. He also said that the DM had requested him to let his father-in-law know that all was well. All this transpired within fifteen days of us returning from Pithoragarh," he smiles. "Ram Kumar called me to ask if everything was satisfactory and I laughed and thanked him."

"I don't know why it is that I sometimes say things spontaneously and they come true," he says. "A similar thing happened with Atal Bihari Bajpayee. I was introduced to him at Mirabai guest house here in Lucknow through a friend of mine named Bhagwati Shukla, who was a Minister in the BJP government. I wanted to meet Vajpayee because I wanted his help in getting another son-in-law transferred out of Assam. Many important people were there at the guest house to meet him, like Lalji Tandon, who was his protégé and a Member of Parliament."

"I told Vajpayee that someone from the Kayastha community had got my son-in-law transferred out of Gorakhpur so that an individual from his community could take over the appointment and that I wanted my son-in-law to be posted back in the state. He hesitated, saying that the two of us were also from the same caste and that it might be considered favouritism if he helped me."

"When I heard this, I said that it was sad that I had been born into the Brahmin community, because, unlike individuals from other communities, Brahmins were reluctant to help out members of their community. Vajpayee considered this for a second and then told me to meet him in Delhi after he returned. I told him that my son-in-law would be the one to meet him in Delhi, but I would certainly meet up with him when he was next in Lucknow."

"Atal Bihari Vajpayee did come through for me. He called up Jaffer Sharief to get my son-in-law transferred back to Lucknow. We met for the second time in Lucknow after the next elections had been announced. I had carried a horde of cash with me in my Jeep, which I handed over to him after I thanked him. I said without thinking that it was untainted money and would prove lucky for him. Taking me into the bedroom, he placed the money in his briefcase, assuring me that he would treasure it. I also left my Jeep with him, saying that it would be useful for him during the election and that I would reclaim it after he had won the election."

"Atal Bihari Vajpayee won the election and became Prime Minister. However, he remained in office only for sixteen days (his second term was for a period of 13 months from 1998 to 1999, followed by a full term from 1999 to 2004). He had to resign because he could not garner enough support to form a government."

"On his next visit to Lucknow, he met me very warmly and said that the money had indeed proved very auspicious for him, even if it wasn't for very long. I said it did not matter: I had brought a second sum of cash with me which would prove to be even more auspicious and he would become Prime Minister again, this time for far longer."

I feel a shiver go down my spine when he says this.

"This happened much before I met with Mayawati, in which I prophesised her becoming Chief Minister," he laughs. "And to think

I may never have met her if it wasn't for the bungalow which she had so desired."

"When my son Ambika was of marriageable age," he says, changing the subject, "I asked my wife to find out if he was interested in any girl so that we would not later be embarrassed after committing to someone else. I had nothing against a love match. After enquiring around, my wife told me that there did not seem to be any particular love interest, and from what she had herself observed, all the boys and girls he knew seemed to have a platonic relationship between them. Well, most of them," he laughs. "There was this daughter of a Member of Parliament who had a serious crush on my son. Desperate for his attention, she banged her car into his one day, but her hopes of getting to know him that way came to naught."

"There was a very wealthy liquor dealer who was interested in marrying his only daughter to my son and he told me that if I agreed, he would send over a DCM vehicle laden with currency notes for me. I told him that I was not interested and that I believed that wealth should always be earned through honest means and hard work."

"After this, there was another proposal from a person in Delhi, who had his own air cargo company. He also had an only daughter. His wife and he even came to visit us in Lucknow. We told our friend V.N. Mishra, who was the Director General of Police, to enquire about the antecedents of the girl. But before he could do so, he met up with his friend Pramod Tiwari at the Boat House Club in Nainital and told him about the proposal. Pramod questioned him about our family and then asked why they couldn't get his elder daughter married to the boy instead. V. N. Mishra told him that the boy's family was excellent and it would have been a great idea except for the fact that our families were culturally very different. Pramod was undeterred and told him to go ahead with it anyway."

"When V. N. Mishra discussed the idea with me, I also hesitated, saying that it was a political family and I did not know if my son and his daughter would be a good match. V. N. Mishra said that he could vouch for the girl and that she would make an excellent wife for my son."

"Since I respected his opinion a lot, I agreed to a meeting between my son and Pramod's daughter. Ambika went to meet the girl accompanied by my elder daughter. Aradhana, Pramod's daughter, was accompanied by their family friend Ratna Singh, who was a Member of Parliament."

I am impressed to learn that Uncle had been liberal enough to allow the boy and girl to meet without either of the parents being present.

"The boy and the girl liked each other, so Pramod asked to come over to our house to meet us. At the time, this bungalow was still being renovated and the living room was in shambles. The only seating was broken-down wicker chairs in the hall. My wife was unperturbed by this and said if the girl's father disregarded the condition of our home, it would tell her that he was astute and discerning and that was the kind of person we were interested in having a lifelong association with."

"Pramod came over to our house accompanied by Ratna Singh and Akhilesh Das, who later became the Chief Minister of Uttar Pradesh and told us he was very keen on the alliance. My wife still had apprehensions, telling V. N. Mishra that we were very simple folk and she hoped that the girl, raised in an affluent and renowned political family, would be able to adjust to us. He assured her that she didn't need to worry."

"The engagement and wedding followed soon after the meeting. The wedding was grand and seventeen planes landed in Lucknow with wedding guests. But my youngest daughter's wedding was even grander and was graced by more dignitaries than my son's wedding. The Governor and the Chief Minister attended her wedding, but they had to walk the entire length of the drive because cars were not allowed inside!"

There is a long pause in the conversation as we both sip coffee and since he has been talking about the children, I ask if he spent a lot of time with them while they were growing up. I do have an idea that he probably did not, because of the newspaper article he had shown me in the very beginning, in which he had shared that he regretted not being closer to his children.

"No, I did not" he replies truthfully. "All my life, the centre of my Universe was just my wife and although I may have been a good father in terms of providing for my children, I was not overly affectionate or indulgent towards them."

I think that being such a good provider for his own and extended family as well as the family of his wife, providing all of them with the opportunity and resources to succeed in life, more than compensated for overt displays of love.

"So what has been the biggest achievement of your life, Uncle?" I question him.

"My greatest achievement has been the respect I have received from society at large and the Brahmin community in particular. Recently, I accompanied my friend from Bombay to the house of a gentleman named Ashok Bajpayee, who is also a Member of Parliament. Ashok told my friend that he was very honoured to have me in his house, as I was greatly venerated by the Brahmin community. Rajesh Singh, the owner of Hotel Paradise, echoed the same thing when I went over to his house to assist him in some matter. He told his guests that he was greatly indebted to B.C. Mishra for having graced his house with his presence, as I was not known to make casual visits. He also remarked to my embarrassment that even the saintliest of persons had some flaws, but he had yet to see any in me and he had not come across any person who had a single disparaging thing to say about me. I was extremely humbled to hear these words."

"Pramod once remarked that I was so respected because I had never wavered from my word or my principles and cited an incident from 1977 when I attended a Brahmin Samaj meeting in Sarkarita Bhawan. The discussion had predominantly been about the ills of dowry. I told the gathering that the platitudes did not count as they differentiated between their sons and daughters when it came to dowry and were only too happy to receive it. I said I had pledged to never take a rupee in dowry and asked them to pledge the same."

"Hari Shankar Tiwari, an erstwhile Ganglord who later became a member of the legislature was present at this convocation. At my son's wedding, he came up to me and told me that he was impressed that I had indeed honoured my pledge."

DEHLEEZ

Summer has given way to winter and Uncle is wearing a silver-gray puffer jacket today. It suits his fair complexion and I once again reflect on his good looks and charisma and how much more attractive he must have been in his youth: the young Krishna to his hordes of admiring Gopis.

The book is coming to a close and although I have taken long enough over it, I have mixed feelings about its ending. It has been a remarkable and poignant journey.

Uncle seems to be in a sentimental mood as well and starts with a couplet:

"Mohabbat ki dor itni tagdi hai
Ki Khuda bhi use tod na saka"
(The bond of love is so strong
That even God could not break it)

He tells me that these were the first words he uttered to his nephew when he recovered from his month-long ordeal in hospital in January 2014.

"I miss the raunak (bustle) that used to be in the house when she was alive; the sound of music and laughter and the presence of the clothes and jewellery sellers. The evenings are especially lonely for me, despite all the people in the house. When she was alive, we would watch television together at night. I have not switched it on since she passed away. A few days ago, my son came and turned it on for me in the evening, but I switched it off after he left the room."

"The other night, and I have hesitated in sharing this with you, my wife's photograph fell suddenly from the wall and the frame got a bit damaged. My grandson placed the photograph on the bed in the inner room to get it repaired. Later that night, while going to the toilet, I looked at the photograph on the bed and I felt that it was her lying there in the cold. I went and fetched a blanket and covered her photograph with it. I am sharing a very personal moment of weakness with you," he trails off.

I am choked with emotion, much more than at any other point in the book, including him glimpsing Aunty's face in the rearview mirror after their wedding and then seeing her in the green sari with her long wet hair. If ever true love has existed, I think, this is it.

He proves this further when he says, "I did not know her before I got married to her, so I fell in love with her after, and our love lasted sixty-two years."

From where does a boy who fled his home at the age of thirteen and never really spent time with family get these values and emotions?

Uncle goes into the inner room and emerges with a picture I have not seen before. It is of both of them with their two youngest children, obviously taken somewhere on vacation. "Turn it towards the light so that you can see her better," he tells me.

Aunty looks like a girl in the picture, but Uncle tells me that she was forty-two when the picture was taken. I look at her with reverence for some time before handing the picture back to him.

"Like Madhubala, she never did any makeup in her life," he says, still enamoured with his partner who is no more. "And she never wore heels."

"How tall was she?" I ask, and he tells me, not unsurprisingly, because all their children are very tall; that she was five feet seven.

I tell him he looks dashing in the picture, upon which he is quiet for a while, and then says that there is an incident from his youth which he has never mentioned to me because it is inconsequential and also embarrassing, but he feels he can share it with me now. "You can include it in the book if you want to," he adds.

"When I was staying with my sister in Bareilley, her sister-in-law visited them and took quite a shine to me. Although I was aware of my looks and bearing, I was still quite shy. One day, she announced that she wanted to go shopping. The market was about ten kilometres away and she asked me to accompany her. I refused. She then went to her brother and persuaded him to tell me to go with her. I could not refuse my brother-in-law. A rickshaw was ordered for us and we left for the market in it. She sat smugly as if she had won a prize, while I squeezed myself as far away from her as possible. She probably expected that we would roam around like a couple in the market, but I chose to follow her at a distance of at least fifteen feet. She was very annoyed but did not give up. When the shopping was done, she declared that she wanted to watch a movie with me. I flatly refused to do this and she sat down like a petulant child on the sidewalk, saying she would not budge from there until I complied. After a great deal of persuasion, I was finally able to convince her to come home. She never spoke to me again."

I wonder what was so embarrassing about this rather sweet and amusing anecdote that Uncle could not share it with me earlier. I ask mischievously if he has any more such stories to share, and he shyly replies that there may have been more instances like this one, but he does not remember them.

"There is a funny incident that I remember from childhood, though," he says, clearly wanting to steer the conversation away from any more embarrassing incidents. "When I was ten years old, there was a wedding at my sister's house in the village. Carpets and sheets had been put outside for the guests to sleep on, as was the norm in the village those days. Suddenly, it began to rain. I quickly rolled up the carpet I was sleeping on and took it inside, where I dropped it on the floor. We heard yelps coming from inside the carpet and when I opened it, we discovered that there was a dog inside it! I think it was sleeping with me, probably using me as a pillow!"

I laugh loudly at this, imagining the fright of the poor dog.

Uncle's phone rings and he starts speaking to the caller. He is not very happy with whatever he is hearing, because he says, 'We don't have anything to do with them anymore,' and 'Yes, they are influential. So what? They will have to pay.' He then ends the conversation by telling the caller, 'You know that threats have never mattered to me.'

Then, emerging suddenly from his persona of the strongman, he says that when his wife's body was on the bier, he applied vermillion in the parting of her hair because it is the mark of a married woman. "Unfortunately, I lost the picture that someone took of the moment." Then he recites these lines:

"Umr ka badhna toh dastoore jahan hai
Mehsoos na karein toh badhti kahan hai
Umr ko agar harana hai toh
Shauk zinda rakhiye
Ghutne chalein ya na chalein
Mann udta parinda rakhiye
Mushkilon ka aana toh part of life hai
Aur unme has ke bahar aana
Yehi Art of Life hai"

(Old age is destined
One must experience every moment of life
If one wishes to stay young
One must not give up on experiences
One's body may not be able
But one's mind can always be in flight
Hardships are part of life
And to come out smilingly from them
That is the Art of Life)

"Throughout our lives, my wife and I worked very hard and we never thought of quitting. Maybe that is why the ravages of age never showed on our faces," he says and turns towards his wife's photograph on the wall. I realize for the first time that she is not wearing any jewellery in it, as the occasion of her son's wedding warranted.

"A lot of famous women had plastic surgery back in the day, which is why they managed to continue to look beautiful despite their age, but in my wife's case, it was all-natural," he says.

"Which famous women?" I ask curiously, and he names some of them. "Really?" I ask and tell him I am surprised that these women felt the need for it despite their great achievements and successes. "Well, everyone has their weaknesses," he says.

"So what is yours?" I question with a smile.

He thinks for a moment and then says that he is very sentimental and sensitive inside, but could never show it. "No child of mine has ever embraced me or touched me," he says almost regretfully.

"But you did quite alright by your five children," I tell him. He says that there were not five children, but six.

"Six!" I exclaimed, wondering if another child had died in infancy.

"My wife brought her brother's daughter to live with us when she was a toddler and she never went back to her family. We were the ones to raise her and finally get her married."

I am stupefied. I already know of the three brothers-in-law he raised like his own sons, but we are about to finish the book and I have just learned about another person who was raised in their home!

"How come you never mentioned this before, Uncle?" I ask. "Well, Aunty was always doing this kind of thing," he answers as if it isn't a big deal at all. "Even my eldest daughter's son grew up in our house and we were the ones who got him married. His marriage took place before the marriage of our third daughter."

I shake my head in disbelief.

"She was so loving, generous, and patient," he tells me, completely discounting himself and giving all the credit to his wife. "She would always listen to people's stories and empathise with them and do whatever she could to help."

"We undertook many pilgrimages together and had splendid darshans (auspicious sight of a deity) of the kind that are accorded to celebrities. Once, we saw a telecast of a famous actor couple who visited the shrine of Tirupati Balaji after they got married (the most popular legend associated with this temple is that it is the abode of Lord Vishnu, who will guide his devotees to the end of the present Kali-yuga age). It showed them having a long, private darshan of the deity while thousands of common people waited outside for just a glimpse. We had both remarked enviously that a VVIP status could even help one in getting closer to God. I didn't know that one day we would have a better darshan than the actor couple, till we visited the temple of Tirupati Balaji along with our daughter-in-law and were led into the innermost recess, further on from the gallery where the actor couple had been seated."

"Wow!" I exclaim, aware that the temple is one of the most visited pilgrimage sites and one has to make prior bookings even to wait in lines to enter the temple.

"Someone close to me knew the Chairman of the Tirupati Balaji Trust. He was the one who arranged for us to spend almost an hour in the inner recess, right next to the deity, and even watch the idol being bathed and dressed," he explains.

"Another pilgrimage that we took was to Gangasagar, about which it is said 'Sab Tirth Bar Bar Ganga Sagar Ekbar,' meaning one may visit other holy places several times in one's lifetime, but one visit to Gangasagar is worth a lifetime. Perhaps it is because the journey is so arduous, undertaken in three parts over both land and sea. It is located at a distance of 135 km from Calcutta but is not directly connected to the city and one needs to board a bus first for the port of Kakdwip; a journey of three hours. From Kakdwip, one has to take a crowded ferry to the island of Sagardwip where the holy river Ganges meets the ocean. Then one has to travel in a Tempo or bus to the Kapil Muni shrine, which is venerated by millions over the globe who congregate there on the auspicious occasion of Makar Sankranti in search of Moksha. The Gangasagar Mela is the world's second-largest human congregation at the place where the Ganges meets the Bay of Bengal after the Kumbh in Allahabad."

"We had booked a flight to Calcutta, but because of heavy rains, our flight got cancelled. Then our daughter-in-law informed us that there was a flight available to Delhi and from Delhi to Calcutta. I told her to book both flights at once. When we disembarked from the plane at Calcutta airport, there was a bevy of policemen waiting for us. I was startled when I heard them asking for me, but they were there on the orders of the Director General of Police of West Bengal, who had directed them to escort us to the temple."

"It was Pramod who had contacted the DGP without telling us. He told him that his daughter's in-laws were flying to Calcutta for the pilgrimage to Gangasagar and they should be well looked after."

"A convoy of police vehicles led us from the airport right up to the shore from where steamers took pilgrims to the temple. On the way, we must have passed lakhs of pilgrims. At the shore, a special steamer with seven or eight policemen was waiting to ferry us to the island."

"Once at the island, we expected to have to walk through the marsh to reach the tempos which would take us to the shrine, but there was another police vehicle waiting there to drive us right up to the shores of the shrine. We zipped through the many barricades used for controlling the throngs of pilgrims. That was not all. Near the shrine, there are two cottages for the Chief Secretary and the DGP of the state. We were taken to the DGP's cottage to rest and freshen up and when we finally walked the short distance to the shrine, it was over the jute mats that they had placed so that we would not wet our feet! And while most pilgrims can only enter the lower portion of the shrine, we were taken right to the top of it, where we were as close to the deity as we could be."

"Another memorable pilgrimage was to Mallikarjuna Temple, one of the twelve Jyothirlingas of Lord Shiva." (Mallikarjuna is a Hindu temple dedicated to the deity Shiva, located at Srisailam in the state of Andhra Pradesh. Here, the goddess Parvati is worshiped as 'Mallika' and Lord Shiva is worshipped as 'Arjuna', represented by the lingam; a phallus-shaped symbol of the divine generative energy of the God Shiva.)

The word Jyothirlinga makes me start. It has a mention in my second book, 'The Last Pilgrims,' a memoir of the tragedy that befell my parents. Just before they undertook their last pilgrimage to the Kedarnath shrine also dedicated to Lord Shiva, my father had spent two years travelling to all twelve Jyothirlingas and the four Dhams of the Hindu faith. Jyothirlingas are devotional representations of Shiva. The word is a Sanskrit compound of 'Jyotis,' meaning radiance, and 'Linga,' or Lingam. The Char Dham (literally; four abodes) is a set of four pilgrimage sites which every Hindu is supposed to visit during one's lifetime to attain salvation.

"We reached Hyderabad, from where a deputation of security vehicles of the Labour Minister of Andhra Pradesh took us to the temple situated about two hundred kilometres away in the Nallamala forest, which was overrun by terrorists. There too, the last leg of the journey is supposed to be on foot through marshy land created by the river Krishna. The convoy led us straight to the guest house belonging to the temple, where we changed our clothes for the Rudra Puja (a set of mantras to invoke and pay obeisance to the Shiva tattva: the energy of Shiva in the cosmos, which is said to not only help one grow spiritually but also attain everything in the material world)."

A servant walks into the room with a platter of boiled water chestnuts. I have never eaten boiled water chestnuts and I am surprised to learn that they are delicious.

"We also went to Kedarnath twice (I try not to wince at the mention of the place where my parents breathed their last). The first time was in the 1980s when a group of us comprising thirty-six family members and friends visited it for the first time. There was barely even a town there then. We toured the whole of Uttarakhand on that trip. All the arrangements were made by my brother-in-law, whom I had helped in getting employment with the Department of Irrigation. In Rudraprayag, we stayed in a government guest house at the confluence of the Alaknanda and Mandakini rivers. In Kausani, we stayed where the President of India had once stayed and from the dining room, we had a hugely panoramic view of Trishul, Nanda Devi, Panchachuli, and other majestic Himalayan peaks."

"Our next trip to Kedarnath was in 2005 when we also trekked to Badrinath, Yamunotri, and Gangotri."

"Where else have you travelled, Uncle?" I ask, quite intrigued at the detailed account of his travels.

"Cheerapunji," he replies, the place which has often been credited as being the wettest place on earth. "The AGM of Northern Railways was my son-in-law's elder brother and he told us that we should visit Kamakhya (the Kamakhya Temple at Nilachal hills in Guwahati, Assam is one of the oldest and most revered centres of Tantric practices) and that he would make all the arrangements for the visit. He booked a dedicated coach for us in the Rajdhani train to Guwahati and since my wife did not like to eat outside food, a separate pantry car was attached to the coach, where our servant Raju did all the cooking for us on the journey. After a splendid visit to Kamakhya, where priests from Indian Railways gave us special treatment, we went on to Cheerapunji. On the same trip, we also went to Kaziranga National Park in Assam."

"Then there was a week-long trip to Rishikesh with the whole family. We stayed at a beautiful spot fifteen kilometres above Rishikesh. We also travelled to Nepal to visit the famous Pashupatinath temple and the Devi ka mandir in Pokhra, where eggs are offered to the deity."

At the mention of Nepal, I asked if he ever went to the casinos there, not expecting him in the least to reply in the affirmative.

"But of course!" he replies, to my great surprise. Or maybe I should not be surprised, because my protagonist is a staunch Brahmin who has smoked cigarettes, drunk liquor, and eaten eggs and fish. What is a mere casino? I can't help laughing in admiration and I tell him why I am laughing. He remains nonchalant and unwittingly adds to the admiration when he tells me that when they visited Hardwar (Haridwar, or the 'Gateway to the Gods', is located where the river Ganges enters the Indo-Gangetic plains and is also one of the holiest pilgrimage towns), they drank and ate meat on the VIP Ghat (flight of steps leading to the river) there.

"But one cannot even procure liquor in Hardwar!" I exclaim. Hardwar is a strictly vegetarian town and liquor is also strictly prohibited. He only smiles and shrugs in response.

I must mention here about the writer Donald Robertson who came up with the hypothetical ideal of a 'Stoic Sage,' whom he describes thus:

'The Sage is supremely virtuous, a perfect human being, and the closest mortal approximation to Zeus. He is a completely good person, who lives a completely good and 'smoothly flowing' life of total serenity; he has attained perfect happiness and fulfillment (eudaimonia). He lives in total harmony with himself, the rest of mankind, and Nature as a whole, because he follows reason and accepts his fate graciously, insofar as it is beyond his control. He has risen above irrational desires and emotions, to achieve peace of mind. Though he prefers to live as long as it is appropriate and enjoys the 'festival' of life, he is completely unafraid of his death. He possesses supreme practical wisdom, justice, benevolence, courage, and self-discipline. His character is praiseworthy, honourable and beautiful.'

I feel as if I am sitting in front of the human form of that hypothetical ideal.

My Stoic Sage continues with his saga: "Out of the twelve Jyothirlingas and the four Dhams, only three remained till last year: Somnath, Dwarika, and Nageshwar, and my wife wanted to visit them all. However, she was not keeping well and we decided to only visit Dwarika, although the journey seemed formidable. Once again, our friends helped us out. The Police Commissioner of Lucknow said his batch mate was posted in Dwarika and he would make us as comfortable as possible. True to his word, we had policemen escort us throughout and we did not have to wait in queue anywhere. My wife was even provided a wheelchair, which was taken right up to the idol in the temple. The temple, which usually opens in the evening, was also opened up for us in the afternoon."

"We were able to do Somnath and Nageshwar as well. In Somnath, the last kilometre of the journey is invariably on foot. For us, however, a vehicle of the Somnath Trust had been arranged. When we disembarked to start ascending the steps to the temple, they took us to the side of the temple which had a door that led to an elevator! The elevator led us right to the idol in the temple!" He laughs at the memory and then says softly that it was their last pilgrimage together. "We went in February and she was gone in November."

We are both silent for a while. I think of something to say which will lift the gloom in the room. Finally, I asked him what deity he believes in the most, and expectedly, he said he does not believe in any deity but does have faith in all three forms of the Goddess Durga: Mahalakshmi, Mahakali, and Mahasaraswati; whom he believes helped him through all the obstacles in life.

"Even as we prospered, we never became arrogant or greedy and never turned away any needy person. Over the years, countless people came to us from our village and even neighbouring villages for help. Sesendi has come to be known as Ambalika because of the name of our Engineering and Management College and auto drivers and passengers refer to it as such. It still feels so strange, because I have not forgotten the day that we went to the Raja of Sesendi's house to wish him on Holi and he did not even get up to greet me. I may have been a common man then unlike the Raja, but I always believed that Holi was a festival where one embraced all, irrespective of status. I have never treated any member of my staff or any underling as beneath me."

"Four or five years ago, we made a deal to sell one of our houses in Gomtinagar for two crore rupees. The buyer gave me an advance of five thousand rupees but did not cough up the rest of the money owed to me. A year passed and the price of the property escalated to three and a half crores. I could have easily got out of the deal and made a handsome profit, but I have always felt that one should honour one's word and so I preferred a loss of a crore and a half rupees rather than renege on my word."

At this point, I am no longer surprised to hear of my subject's philanthropy.

"What was your relationship like with your brothers and sisters in later years?" I ask him and he describes how his eldest sister remained estranged from him for many years while the younger sister remained estranged from their eldest brother who had ousted him from their house with his wife and infant daughter. However, at the time of Janeu (Janeu is a consecrated thread that is worn by every Hindu Brahmin of India. This holy thread suggests the development of a male from a young boy to a man) of his younger sister's son, he convinced his eldest brother to come and perform the duties of elder brother at the ceremony.

I question him about how he could find it in himself to forgive those who had harmed him and even go out of his way to help them and he says, "It is important to nurture relationships. And after all, what was I supposed to do: fight with my own family, while looking out for countless others who weren't even related to me? I have told you about my friend V. N. Mishra, the Inspector General of Police who came with me to the police station in the Manager case. I gave up land worth ten crores to him simply because he helped me out in my time of need. I had bought some land a few years before this incident and put twenty bighas of it in his name, telling him that we would eventually divide it between us. After this incident happened, I gave him the entire twenty bighas, which were worth ten crores. He refused saying that it was not what we had decided on, but I told him that what he had done for me was far greater than any monetary value."

"Doctor Chandravati, whom I had helped with the squatters, was the one who operated on my daughter Pinky (Meenakshi) in Queen Mary Hospital in 1980," he recounts with a sad smile. "At the time of Pinky's surgery, the hospital parking was not big enough to accommodate all the vehicles of our high-profile visitors. My aide went to fetch me a coffee from the vendor in the hospital and was asked if he knew who the VIP was for whom all the important visitors had been coming to the hospital. My aide decided to have some fun with him and he said that it was his boss, a Mafia Kingpin, which is why top criminals were visiting him while all the police and officials were there to try and catch him. The coffee vendor became so nervous at hearing this that he nearly spilled the coffee and refused to let the aide pay for it. The aide returned and told me the story. I felt sorry for the poor vendor and told the aide to go and tell him that it was a joke and to pay him his money. The coffee vendor would still not take the money and an Inspector of Police had to be sent to reassure him that the aide was indeed joking."

Except he wasn't, not entirely, I smile inwardly.

I can't help drawing parallels between the unwitting hero of my book and the 'Givers' in the book 'Give and Take' by Adam Grant of the Wharton School of Business, where he distinguishes between Givers, Takers, and Matchers in terms of their 'reciprocity styles' and argues that Givers are the most successful across many industries. Givers, he says, often put the needs and interests of others above their own. Takers almost always put themselves first in their interactions with others. Matchers strive to keep an equal balance of giving and getting. While many people are Givers in their close relationships, they become Matchers and even Takers in work contexts. But true Givers focus on acting in the interest of others by giving help, mentoring, sharing credit, or making connections for others without engaging in heroic deeds or extreme self-sacrifice.

As I silently bless the Giver in front of me for all his altruism and philanthropy, he goes on, "Around the time of my son's wedding, I faced another financial crisis. We had spent a whole lot of money on our very extravagant weddings. I sold one of our farms in Kanpur for twenty-two lakhs and asked our family priest in Kanpur whether I needed to start being prudent with money. He told me that I would never need to be prudent with money and that money would always find its way to me if I did not think about it too much."

"So I bought more land," he says, while I look at him with astonishment. "Our financial situation became worse. My wife and I went to Kanpur once again to meet the priest. 'What advice did you give me?' I asked him. 'It has made my situation worse.' The priest was unperturbed and told me he had only stated what he knew for a fact: that there were no money problems in our fate lines. He said that I should not worry about money because I would never suffer disgrace because of it. We came back to Lucknow but I remained tense about my situation, especially since I owed a fairly large sum of money which I had to repay in four days. My wife and I were so anxious that we went to bed without eating dinner."

"The next morning, the children came into our room to have morning tea with us as they always did. They left after that but Ambika returned to ask me if I had secured the money. 'What money?' I asked him. 'The money that the gentleman from Noida left for you to invest as you wish,' he replied, and seeing my puzzlement, told me that it was in a bag under my bed. I pulled out the bag and saw that it contained a large sum of money!"

"I only needed four or five lakhs to repay my debt," Uncle continues, "So things worked out the way the priest had predicted they would. Till today, I have never faced insolvency, even during the terrible pandemic, which put many companies out of business."

"The priest was a famous tantric whom even Indira Gandhi would consult from time to time. He once saw famous personalities like the Raja of Amethi, the Raja of Killoi, Sanjay Singh, and Ratna Singh at our house and told me that although all of them had royal lineage, it was I who was living like a King and would continue to do so if I did not worry about debts and other problems."

"Around thirty years ago, he handed me two bundles of notes: one of five hundred rupee notes and the other of two thousand rupees and told me to keep them safely with me, saying I would never lack money if I did so. I still have those notes."

"After that, I started giving him a sum of money each month: five thousand to fifty thousand rupees; whatever I could spare at the time. When his daughters got married, my wife bought their entire jewellery for them. I could never have thought that the people who could not afford to get back their own mortgaged jewellery would one day be able to buy so much of it for others."

"Was this the same priest who once told you that you would own a fleet of cars?" I ask, and he replies that it was. "Is he alive?" I ask him hopefully. "No, he died in our house in 2001, just after the marriage of my son. When we were matching the astrological charts of my son and daughter-in-law, he said that although the match was favourable, some elderly people on both sides would pass away after the wedding. I was shocked and wanted to call off the wedding, but he told me that it would be old grandparents on the girl's side and since he was the eldest person on my side of the family, it would be him who would bear the brunt of the prophecy. He urged me to go ahead with the marriage. I didn't believe him, but a year after the wedding, he did indeed pass away in our house."

Is there no end to the list of incredible stories my protagonist has to share, I wonder, as I mull over the supreme sacrifice of the priest.

"While we were still in the Rajendarnagar house, it was he who had prophesized that we would leave that house to go and live in a house in ruins. This had worried us and although I had paid the advance for a bungalow in the cantonment, I decided that we would not buy it. 'It will not make any difference,' the priest laughed when he was told about my change of plans. 'You will move, whether you like it or not, into this bungalow or another, and the house will look like a ruin.'

I had seen a photograph of their bungalow which was taken before the family shifted into it and it had indeed looked like a ruin in it: derelict and ghostly. I wished the family priest was alive. I would have loved to meet him to get some prophesies of my own.

"It was in 2001 that I started my construction machinery rental business. Like the Chit Fund and the Transport and Real Estate business, it was hugely successful. I bought a hundred and fifty JCBs, Piling Rigs, Dumpers, Loaders, and Concrete Mixers and started sending them to construction sites all over the country. My rental revenue from this business alone was about a crore and half rupees a month."

It is hard for me to imagine such large sums of money back then. "So all your business ventures proved to be very lucrative, right, Uncle?" I ask.

To my surprise, he replies "Not exactly," and tells me about some which were not so successful. "I once set up a sand mining business and a stone-crushing business, but both failed. I also set up a Piling Rig in partnership with a friend, which was also unsuccessful."

"We also set up a resort next to my farmhouse, but that also did not work out for many reasons. For years, I had held parties every week at the farmhouse, sometimes for up to a hundred people, where the liquor would be flowing and sumptuous banquets were laid out with special dishes of chicken and fish brought in from renowned restaurants in

Lucknow; I suppose people expected things would continue the same way at the resort. Then, some of these people also started misusing the resort for unscrupulous activities, if you know what I mean. That is where I drew the line and closed down the resort. Even for the farmhouse parties, there had always been strict instructions for my staff to not allow anyone to spend the night there and inebriated guests would be escorted to their cars and sent off."

"I was very addicted to paan masala at one time, as I have told you, but in 1995, I left it once and for all and never touched it again, not even when my wife would get back sweet paans for the family. When I gave it up, I started getting dizzy spells because of nicotine withdrawal, but I had resolved not to touch any tobacco product again. With this last vice gone from my life, I became less and less interested in the get-togethers at the farmhouse and then finally stopped attending them, although they carried on for many years without me! Plus, the crowd at the parties was mostly very senior officials and I did not want my three sons-in-law to feel awkward at their father-in-law's parties while he mingled with their seniors."

I am amazed at both his willpower and his frankness. He left cigarettes and alcohol at his wife's behest soon after his wedding, even though he had been smoking five packets of cigarettes every day for three or four years. Then he also managed to kick the paan masala habit and was never even tempted to go back to it. And with all his power and influence, he still preferred to be a family man who spent all his time in the company of his wife.

"We also started a Go Karting track at the spot where the College now stands. It was also in partnership with someone and perhaps if we had gone at it alone, we would not have suffered big losses on it. The partner was irresponsible and we had to bear the expenses for his many extravagances even before the project got underway. Plus, the project was also probably ahead of its time."

"Do you have any regrets in life, Uncle?" I ask.

"Yes," he says but adds that even though there may be things one feels regretful about, a man who mires himself in regret cannot progress.

"The body gets old, but it gets older with worry. If the mind remains strong, it reflects on the body."

"All decisions would be taken jointly by my wife and me. She always knew what was going on with the businesses and would discuss everything with my son and me in the evening when we returned home."

"We were known to be quite mute in her presence," he laughs. "Everyone knew that we could still be made to change our minds, but once she took a decision, she would not go back from it."

"My trucks used to mostly ply on two routes: Bihar-Bengal and Jhansi. I knew all the cops and RTO officials along these two routes and that helped in solving a lot of problems that arise in this business. One foggy night, six of my trucks met with accidents between Calcutta and Benares. Six men died in these accidents. I handled the post mortems of all six men and handed over the bodies to their families, compensating them handsomely for their loss. Witnessing their grief was heart-wrenching. But what was most heart-wrenching was the scene I witnessed when I drove out in the middle of the night to one of the accident sites in Barabanki close to Lucknow. The truck with its cargo of tea chests was overturned. A crane was already there to upright the truck. While this was being done, the dead body of the driver fell out of the window and onto the road. I have never experienced a more traumatic thing than this, although all the accident sites were horrific. I drove to all of them one by one. At Kanpur, the truck was carrying gravel and the driver had allowed twenty people to ride on top of it. When the accident happened, they were toppled over and buried under the gravel."

"Did they all die?" I ask, horrified. "No," he laughs at my horrified expression, "We had to unearth them, but they were all alive."

"At the accident near Malliabagh, the driver and conductor both survived and were admitted into the hospital there. I drove out to the site and my wife drove to the hospital. She reported to me that the driver was critical and they feared for his life, but the conductor was not badly injured and would probably survive, although he was complaining of great pain. The next day, I also drove to the hospital to check on them and was shocked to learn that the conductor had passed away because of an injury to his kidney, but the driver had survived the night and was going to recover. He remained in the hospital for three months. We took the conductor's body back to his family."

"That night is hard to forget, although minor accidents were common enough. The financial loss was big, but the heartache was far bigger."

Then he quotes these lines:

"Aksar main tolta rehta hoon
Kuch chehre, kuch baatein
Kuch bhooli bisri yaadein
Dhoond rahi hain mujhe
Kya sahi tha, kya galat tha
Pooch rahi hain mujhse
Umr ke saath saath soch badalti rehti hai
Chahat badalti rehti hai, khoj badalti rehti hai
Ab iss mukam pe therav aa gaya hai
Manzil ka toh pata nahin, par padav aa gaya hai
Bechain man ko rahat milne lagi hai
Samjhauta kar liya toh Zindagi mukammal lagne lagi hai
He Ishwar, tera shukriya, tujhse koi gila shikwa nahin hai
Yahan sab thode adhoore se hain
Kisi ko poora mila hi nahin
Bahut saari kat gayi
Ab thodi si hi bachi hai
Kisi ke hoton pe muskuraoon jaane ke baad bhi
Yaad aoon, bas ab yahi zindagi hai
Yehi Zindagi hai."

(I keep analyzing life, people, memories
What was right and what was wrong
Perspectives change with age
Affections change, goals change
Now I am at a stage in life
Where I do not know the destination
Only that I am at a standstill
But my mind has reconciled
And so I have found peace
I thank you, God
I bear no ill will towards you
There is no perfect fulfillment
Most of my life is over
And now my only wish is to be remembered
With fond memories, with a smile
This is life; this is life)

EPILOGUE

Your life is like this tree, deeply rooted, with a solid foundation and countless branches linking your past throes with future dreams. Every tree faces inevitable storms and strong winds testing the strength of its roots. Branches break; new ones grow. It will flower and leaves will fall. And from your tree, new life will emerge. In the end, though, with purpose and perseverance, your tree will prevail, and each will be beautifully individual and uniquely different. A full circle of such. — Riley Mackenzie

It is strange and serendipitous that this book should end where it started; except that there were no tears in the beginning, just numbness: a grim reality not yet assimilated; and now every eye was moist. The many stages of grief. And how could it be otherwise: we were sitting in the very room where Rama Aunty had lain on her bier when I first saw her, exactly a year ago on the night of Diwali.

I had gone to meet Uncle on Diwali night, aware that it was a very difficult time for all members of the family and wanting to cheer him up a little, if possible. I was relieved to see that the house was lit up and the porch was bedecked with beautiful rangolis made out of yellow and orange marigolds (rangolis are patterns created on the floor using coloured rice, flowers, coloured sand or paints), lamps, and other Diwali accouterments. The day before that had been Uncle's birthday and I had gone over to the house with a cake. The entire family had congregated to celebrate his birthday, although he had not wanted any sort of revelry. It was his first birthday after marriage without his wife. It is hard to imagine exactly what that must feel like after a bond of a lifetime. He was sitting in the living room, handsome as always, with a red tilak (a mark on the forehead associated with certain religious rituals) on his forehead, receiving guests graciously. Bouquets filled the room. I presented Uncle with a draft of the first hundred pages of his biography.

As expected, he did not express any emotion, especially with so many people around. We all had a fabulous lunch indoors and then stepped out for the cake-cutting. But Uncle stepped away to one side and refused to cut the cake. I could see that he was having a difficult time controlling his emotions, especially when a picture of Aunty was brought out by his daughter Mrinalini and daughter-in-law Aradhana and placed near the cake. Uncle's granddaughter, the daughter of Meenakshi who had passed away at a young age, brought out her own two little girls and it was they who finally cut the cake. His son Ambika walked over to him with the first piece of the cake, but he shook his head and did not take it. By now, all his children had tears in their eyes. The eldest daughter Madhulika, at whose birth he had spent the night outside the hospital in a rickshaw, stood far away and it seemed as if she was crying. Malvika, the youngest, stood close by and tried to hide her tears by dabbing at them with the dupatta of the beautiful yellow suit she was wearing. Aradhana stoically sliced up the cake. Mrinalini was unable to hide her tears as she passed plates around to everyone.

Someone suggested taking photographs to commemorate the occasion and we all started congregating around Uncle. He did not object to the photographs, but one could see that he just wanted the celebration to be over and be alone with his memories.

"You've decorated the porch so beautifully, Mona (her nickname)," I told Aradhana. "Bobby didi and I did it," she told me, "because Mummy appeared in my dream last night and asked why her plants were missing from the porch." I looked at the beautiful poinsettias on both sides of the porch steps. "I'm sure she wanted you to decorate the house on Diwali, Mona," I tell her, "And I am glad you did so."

Are some things coincidences or figments of our imagination because that is the way we want them to be, or are the souls of our loved ones never really lost to us? I believe in the latter, even though I follow Buddhist teachings and spirituality.

The Pali word Anatta, which comes from the Sanskrit Anatman, means ''non-self' or 'substanceless,' and Buddhist doctrine believes, unlike the Hindu belief in Atman or self, that there is no permanent, underlying substance in human beings that can be called the soul. It believes that an individual is a compound of five factors (denoted by the word Khandha in Pali or Skandha in Sanskrit*)* that are constantly changing. This concept of Anatta or Anatman; the absence of a self, Anicca (impermanence), and Dukkha (suffering), are the three characteristics of all existence (the Ti-lakkhana) and the realisation of these three doctrines constitutes 'Right understanding.'

However, I have also grown up with the Hindu belief in the immutable or imperishable nature of 'Brahman,' described in the 'Katha Upanisad' as 'the wise one (atman) which is neither born nor dies. It has not come from anywhere and has not become anyone. Unborn, constant, eternal, primeval, it is not slain when the body is slayed.'

And I have to admit, the somewhat nihilistic philosophy of Buddhist doctrine is a lot harder to swallow than the comforting Hindu belief in the indestructibility of the soul, especially when signs start appearing after the death of a loved one, as happened with the family when the Supari (betelnut) tree that was planted by the matriarch of the family flowered for the first time just a few days before Diwali that year; the first year that she would not be with the family.

Uncle's mood was somber that Diwali night. "I started from nothing, and I have ended with nothing," he says. Ambika, Aradhana, and Malvika, who are sitting with us, do not say anything. Feeling sad and awkward, I ask Uncle why he says so. "What do I have today," he answers, "I am as destitute now as I was when I ran away from home at thirteen with only five rupees," but I know that he means a very different kind of destitution.

"Jio toh aise jaise sabhi hamara hai, maro toh aise jaise humara kuch bhi nahen," he says. 'Live as if the whole world is yours and die as if you came with nothing.' I am immediately reminded of the haunting lyrics from my favourite song:

'À ta naissance, tout le monde rit, et tu es le Seul à pleurer

Conduis ta vie de façon à ce qu'à ta mort,

Tout Le monde pleure, et que tu sois le seul à Sourire'

Translated from French, these mean:

'When you are born everyone laughs, and you are the only one to cry

Lead your life so that when you die

Everyone is crying, and you are the one to smile'

"I have kept nothing for myself," he carries on, "and that is the way it should be: what does a man carry to his grave but the legacy of his children?" I agree and tell him that he has a wonderful legacy of loving and obedient children, all of whom are very successful.

"Yes, a man should consider himself lucky when his children do not argue with him and are successful in their own lives."

"And what about all this that you have built and created?" I ask, gesticulating around the room with my hand.

"Wealth is nothing," he says. "Respect is. When my son got married," he says, pointing at him, "I did not take a penny in dowry. People talk about the ills of dowry, but that is only till it comes to their own sons' marriages. I took nothing from my daughter-in-law's family. '*Meri saree, meri gadi, mera zevar*' was my motto (my saree, my car, and my jewellery). I wanted my daughter-in-law to come into my home empty-handed and I should provide everything for her from there on."

At this, Aradhana, who usually refrains from expressing any opinion, speaks up, "I attained Raj Yoga when I married into this family, Papa." (Raj Yoga, according to Hindu astrology, happens when the Trine planets are posited in their own house or exalted. A person with Raj Yoga is said to earn much wealth and fame in his lifetime).

"I was wary of taking a daughter-in-law from a political family," her father-in-law continues, "but many people vouched for the family and her. As I told you, I wielded a lot of political influence in my heyday but never got involved in politics myself, because I thought that politicians were largely corrupt. I will say this for my daughter-in-law's father, though: he was never corrupt. I know of instances where he was offered hefty bribes, but he never accepted them. And I can never forget what he did for me in 2015 when I was hospitalized. He did not leave the side of my bed for seventy-two hours, and neither did my daughter-in-law. He needn't have been there at all, but he chose to be. We often have different viewpoints and our share of arguments, but he always withdraws respectfully after a while."

I have met Aradhana's father, Mr. Pramod Tiwari. He is a powerful man, whose political prowess and flamboyance are no secret to anyone. I am impressed to hear of their mutual respect.

Aradhana asks if I will have dinner and I refuse, but my protestations are disregarded as usual and a dinner plate is placed in front of me. Once again, I cannot refrain from eating the delicious food.

Aradhana and Ambika accompanied me to the car after dinner. While in the driveway, they point to a corner of the garden which is carpeted with fallen yellow flowers from a tree, making the scene look like something out of a fairytale.

The blessings and munificence are evident everywhere: in the yellow and orange marigolds and the red poinsettias on the porch, the flowers and fruit of the betel nut tree, and in the yellow carpet of flowers in the garden which Rama Mishra had loved so much and which Brajesh Mishra and she had cultivated together with so much love and passion.

www.ingramcontent.com/pod-product-compliance
Lightning Source LLC
LaVergne TN
LVHW041215150826
845673LV00001B/414

* 9 7 9 8 8 9 0 6 7 9 9 5 6 *